A KNOWN NOWT'S BETTER THAN AN UNKNOWN NOWT

ROBERT 'BOB' HOLMES

Fisher King Publishing

A Known Nowt's Better than an Unknown Nowt

Copyright © Robert Holmes 2016
ISBN 978-1-910406-29-8

First published in England in 1999

Published by
Fisher King Publishing
The Studio
Arthington Lane
Pool-in-Wharfedale
LS21 1JZ
England
www.fisherkingpublishing.co.uk

DEDICATION

I dedicate this book to my grandchildren Edward
and Robert, my nephew Alan, my niece
Barbara, my nephew Philip and other members
of my family and friends who encouraged me
to put pen to paper.

OLD ADDINGHAM

(not to scale)

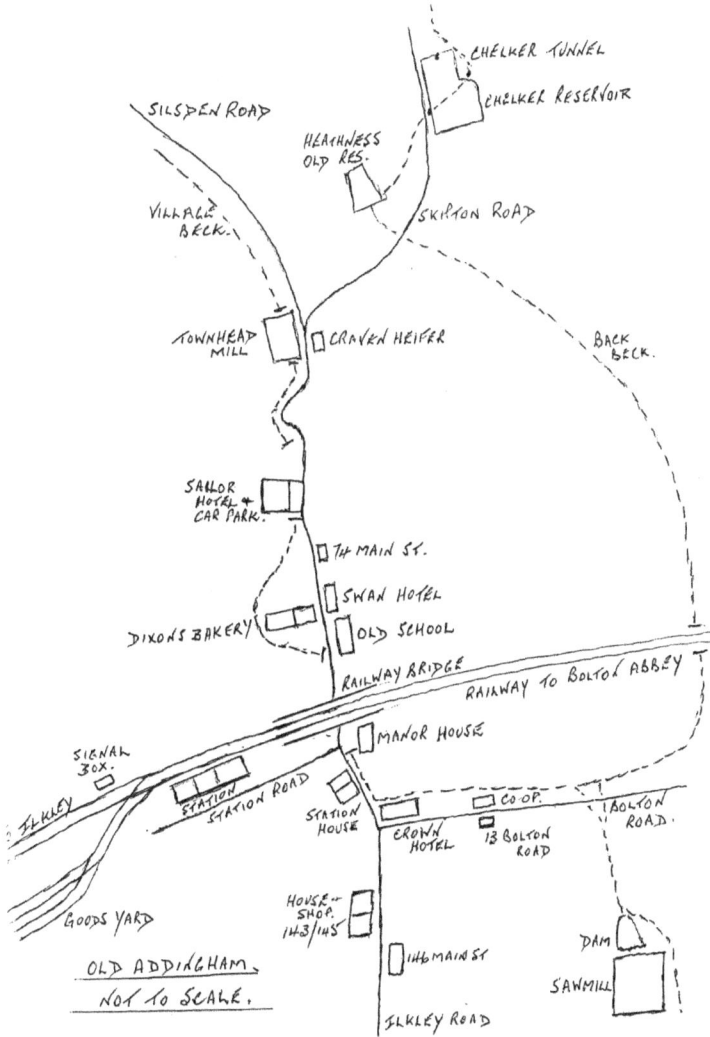

CHELKER TUNNEL

CHELKER RESERVOIR

SILSDEN ROAD

HEATHNESS OLD RES.

SKIPTON ROAD

VILLAGE BECK.

TOWNHEAD MILL

CRAVEN HEIFER

BACK BECK.

SAILOR HOTEL + CAR PARK.

74 MAIN ST.

SWAN HOTEL

DIXONS BAKERY

OLD SCHOOL

RAILWAY BRIDGE

RAILWAY TO BOLTON ABBEY

SIGNAL BOX.

MANOR HOUSE

ILKLEY

STATION ROAD

STATION ROAD

STATION HOUSE

CO-OP.

BOLTON ROAD.

CROWN HOTEL

13 BOLTON ROAD

GOODS YARD

OLD ADDINGHAM. NOT TO SCALE.

HOUSE + SHOP. 143/145

146 MAIN ST

DAM

SAWMILL

ILKLEY ROAD

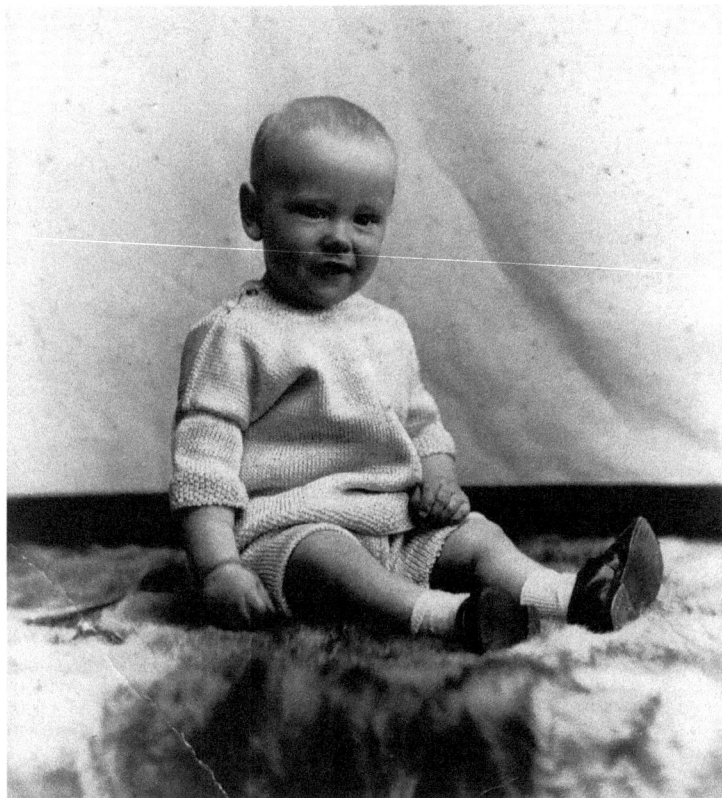

The author, aged one.

FOREWORD

Cricketer, poacher, pigeon fancier

I knew Robert Holmes for over fifty years and was given the pleasure of being one of the first to read his book which brings to light things of which I knew nothing but which make interesting reading.

I knew of his success as a pigeon fancier, both racing and showing, as I have been involved in the same sport learning a great deal from my late father-in-law Walter Horner who kept rabbits and pigeons in out buildings at the Junction Hotel where Robert lived with his father and mother, and was a great exponent of the show scene.

The Holmes family came from Addingham where most of them played cricket for the village team so there was no wonder the lad followed in their footsteps and became good enough to have a trial with Yorkshire County Cricket club - an experience to be proud of.

Anything Robert tackled he did so to perfection and I admired him greatly for that.

Robert Webster

CONTENTS

MY FAMILY BACKGROUND

I was born in Addingham, over the shop at 74 Main Street, on 13 May 1925. My father was Allan Holmes and my mother Maggie Harrison. Note the spelling and names, they are correct, not Margaret, as is so often used.

My father was then thirty-nine and my mother twenty-eight, considered very old at that time for parents having their first child. The reason for this was that they were not allowed to marry young as Allan's brother Fred had married Maggie's sister Eva some years before. In that age it was not considered good for two brothers to marry two sisters. I have never really understood the reasoning behind this old custom.

My father Allan's parents were John Holmes and his wife. John I just remember from when I was a boy of about three or four, but he died about that time. I never knew his wife as she had died many years before. Both are buried at St Peter's Church, Addingham, the graves being inside the west wall, two rows into the churchyard, next to the river in an unmarked plot.

My mother Maggie's parents were James Harrison and Clara Harrison (née Hardisty). Both these grandparents I remember well, often staying with them as a boy at Pace Gate Farm, Beamsley, Bolton Abbey. They were married for over fifty years and I still have the plaque that was presented to them for their golden wedding by his boss, Mr Charlesworth, the owner of Blubberhouses Moor and for whom my grandfather was gamekeeper for many years. My grandfather James died just into the war years and my grandmother during the latter part of the war. Sadly, I did not get to attend their funerals, being away at the time. Both are buried in an unmarked grave at Bolton Abbey Priory Church. This is directly under the point of the east end of the old Priory, and so is one of the most photographed graves in England.

Now just a short reflection on the four most important people to play a part in my early life.

First, my father Allan, he was a hand warp dresser by trade and worked at the Townhead Mill, Addingham all his working life. That is until one day in about 1932 when he was sacked, not made redundant, there was no such thing in those days. In fact, someone had invented a machine to do the same job, and so his trade came to a big full stop. With no redundancy or payments of any kind given to out-of-work people in those days, he had to get work in order to keep his wife and myself. We only had a small amount of income from the sweet shop at 74 Main Street, Addingham, and it would not feed us all. So he went back to what had kept his family years before, working in any job he could find during the day, and poaching at night... we did not starve.

My father was a tall man of six foot, dark haired and of athletic build. A good sportsman in many ways, he played cricket for Addingham First Elevens for many years. At that time they were in the Yorkshire Council, a very good league in those years. He was a good club batsman in his day, and often told me how he had played in many matches for Addingham that contained eleven players with the surname Holmes. Holmes must have been a great sporting family.

To my regret I only played cricket once in the same team as my father, the occasion being an away match with Addingham Firsts at Illingworth, near Halifax, in about 1935. Addingham arrived to play with a man short and I was allowed to play. I do not remember much about the match itself, not even whether we won or lost. However, during the match, my dad was scoring runs freely, but other members of our team kept getting out. At last it came to my turn to bat at number eleven, of course the last man to go in to bat. But the crisis was that dad was forty nine not out and only required one run to get to fifty. This he had to achieve to get a collection from the crowd. So all the other members of our team gave me a stern lecture in the pavilion before going out to bat. Play all the straight balls on the ground so as not to give the chance of a catch, keep your legs out of the way, so not to be out leg before wicket, etc. Plus a hundred other instructions, all this to a lad of ten.

To say this helped in any way, I should think not, only making me even more nervous. However, I did play the over out, stopping three balls and letting the other three go past the wickets knowing they were not straight; I seem to have always had a good eye for things not straight. Dad managed to get the one run required in the next over for his fifty, and so a good collection.

On the way home on the top deck of an old double-decker bus dad counted his pot of cash, it was £7 and 10 shillings, a fortune to him. Wages at the time would only have been about £1 a week for non-tradesman. But the hero of the day was me, with a score of zero not out. I scored many cricket centuries all over the world in later years, but the score of zero not out was the one that mattered when it was surely needed.

Dad was also a good pianist, could play anything and everything by ear and earned a good few tips playing at events and all the local pubs. He was also a great darts player and even today many of the old men tell me about his ability. If darts had been as professional as it is today on television, he would have been among the very best.

He died at The Junction Hotel, Crosshills (now The Dalesway) on 15 March 1942, aged just fifty-six. Then I was only a shy boy of sixteen, an only child, completely lost and totally devastated.

The second person was my mother Maggie Holmes, née Harrison, the third daughter of James and Clara Harrison, who had a family of five surviving children. Clara was the eldest, then Eva, about whom you will hear a great deal later, Wilfred, a son, then Maggie, my mum, and then young James (Jim to all the family) who was the youngest. He was born eighteen years after my mum, Maggie.

Now as my daughter Shirley has so often referred to it, this family was very unusual. Eva was born in 1889, Clara, as I remember, was more than two years older, she could possibly have been more. Mum Maggie was born in July 1897. There was then a gap of almost 18 years prior to Jim, who was born in March 1914. This means that Clara was born in 1886 or earlier, and we know that Jim appeared in 1914. This means a period from first child to last child of at least twenty-eight years, possibly longer. So if my grandmother Clara had been married at sixteen or seventeen, again unusual, she would have had her last child at the age of forty six or indeed could have been nearer fifty.

As far as I know, all the children were born at home at Pace Gate. Medical attention in those days had to be called and then arrived on horseback, meaning that Clara must have been a very fit and healthy woman. I only hope I have some of her genes still in me.

My mum Maggie was a good scholar for where she lived. She had to walk from Pace Gate to Beamsley school and back every day, the journey being three miles one way and the same back at night. She would take only a snack for lunch, and had to endure the terrible weather that blows onto Beamsley and Blubberhouses Moor. But at the end of all this tough and rough time she said she liked school and won prizes for the best attendance. I regret to this day that I failed to follow her example at that early age as far as education went.

Mum was a kind sort of lady and not the bold type of leader. I have found that in many families the first child is nearly always the leader type, and mum was not.

Mum married her second husband during the war and left the district to live in Swinton in South Yorkshire with my stepfather Joe Newham. Whilst away in the war, I received a letter from her while serving in Haifa, Palestine, informing me of what she had done. This came as a great shock to me and was not the news I was expecting; in fact, it confirmed that I had no home to come back to. However, all turned out alright in the end.

Joe Newham died some years later, and in 1961, mum moved back to 145 Main Street, Addingham, next door to our shop at 143 Main Street.

She died on 15 March 1971 and both her and my father Allan are buried in the same grave in Addingham parish churchyard, in the corner under the west wall and the river wall. If you look at this gravestone you will see:

Allan died on the 15th March 1942
Maggie died on the 15th March 1971.

Many people looking at the gravestone think some mistake has been made, but it is correct, both died on the same date twenty-nine years apart.

Now to the other two people who played a great part in my early years: Fred and Eva Holmes.

Fred was my father's older brother and Eva was my mother's older sister. To start with, Fred and Eva were married in 1912, before the First World War, and had been married for over thirteen years when I was born. They never had any children of their own and were my only godparents. In later years they became my second parents when I had nowhere to go after returning from the war in 1947, and they treated me as if I was their own son.

As time passed, people still came up to me and said 'I knew your father and mother'. But they were in fact talking about Fred and Eva, my uncle and aunt. I did not correct them as I thought it was a credit to both of them that no one could tell the difference.

Now Eva had never worked in any special job as people do today, but was always called upon to help with parties and catering events, and years later, when married to Fred, who then worked at the Devonshire Arms, Bolton Abbey, she used to help with all the grouse shooting at the

Estate. These were big events in those days, with Dukes, Duchesses, Lords, Ladies and even the King coming to shoot grouse on the 12 August opening of the season. She had served them all many times.

She was a slim, dark-haired lady, not as good a scholar as her sister, my mother, but she had a style, flair and presentation that not many country girls had. Eva had it all and used it to great advantage when going into business at the Crown Hotel with husband Fred in 1933. To sum up, she was a woman of style and something that many women can only aspire too even today.

Now just a few words about my Uncle Fred, because later he will be included in many of my stories, some good, some very shady and some hilarious. Fred was a very fit and well-made man, he was only 5' 8" tall and yet weighed nearly fifteen stone, but did not really look that big. Remember, when I went to live with him and Aunt Eva in 1947 he was already sixty-five years old and still as strong as a horse. For example, when the brewery man used to deliver the beer to the Crown, in oak barrels of eighteen gallons, thirty-six gallons or hogsheads of fifty-four gallons, each barrel had to have a brass top knocked into the bung hole ready to connect to the beer pumps. The brewery man used to do this if you required this service, but Fred did his own.

The reason he did this himself was that the brewery men took three or four blows with a wooden mallet to knock the tap in, he did it left-handed in one blow, and therefore never spilt any beer. Yes, he was sixty-five then; think what it would have been like be hit with a left hook like that when he was boxing in the 1920s. I would have been out cold for a month!

To conclude this bit about Uncle Fred, let me say I think he no doubt lived longer because of me. Everyone said he was a father to me, in fact, I know he treated me more like a younger brother. You see he had had a shock with my father's early death and having taught him how to survive in the depression times of the early 20s and 30s without any money.

A poacher in the making.

Fred (left) and Allan (right) Holmes, 1932.

17

After the Second War, he must have thought these times would return, so started teaching me all the old tricks again. Poaching to survive was his password. I will come back to the things I learnt later, but I am sure that for him to go over the old hunting grounds again at almost seventy years of age, did, I am sure, give him a new lease of life.

After Fred and Eva retired they lived in a little cottage in Malt Kiln Yard, Addingham until they died, Fred on December 29 1965, aged eighty-three years; Eva on 12 June 1966, aged seventy-seven years.

Both are buried together in Addingham parish churchyard, on the right-hand side of the pathway leading from the church to the rectory.

During his lifetime, Fred saw the first train go over Addingham Main Street railway bridge in 1888, and the last train in 1965. Not many people would have seen both.

MY EARLY YEARS

I was born above the shop at 74 Main Street, Addingham. The shop had only a small back kitchen, and upstairs a lovely front room as they were called in those days. This had all the usual furniture plus Dad's piano, and it had a nice bay window onto the Main Street from where you could see all goings on up and down the village. I lived in this house for the first eleven years of my life. The activity in the Main Street then, in about 1930, was much greater than it is today; I remember at least fourteen shops selling groceries, four butchers, three fish and chip shops, two banks, a chemist, five pubs, two clubs (Conservative and Liberal), one lemonade factory and five mills still in production and a sawmill.

Next to this bay window mum put a small bed for me in case I was poorly. During the eleven years that I lived there, looking back, I seemed to have spent half of that time in that bed. I had every childhood illness it was possible to have, starting with having to have all my first teeth out because the doctor said the decay was poisoning my system. To follow that I had a string of illnesses that reads more like a medical dictionary. Those that I still remember are diphtheria, measles, mumps, swollen glands or fever, scarlet fever, pneumonia and double pneumonia. No wonder many children in the village died around this time, including some of my very earliest school chums.

However, it was not all bad times; many children's parents were working, many of them in the mill. At holiday times, all the lads such as me were allowed to do as we liked, but not get into any mischief... what a hope!

One of the unusual ways of getting a copper or two to spend was to make the Beck Hunt. This entailed having a pair of wellingtons and a flash light. Then up to and into the village beck above Townhead Mill, follow the beck under the mill and mill yard and Independent Row in Main Street and emerge into daylight for a short distance above the Sailor Hotel. Then continue in the beck under the Sailor car park and out into daylight again. Follow the beck searching for the reward you were looking for under the Main Road opposite the Swan Hotel where the beck takes a sweeping right-hand turn under the old school yard, under G E Carr's shop which stood under the great railway bridge, under the garden of the Manor House and into daylight opposite the station house. The worst was now over as you followed the beck round the bottom of the Garth under Bolton Road and finished behind the saw mill.

Then you would hear the tales of how many rats had been encountered on the journey, and to hear some of the lads you would have thought the rats had grown to the size of tomcats.

We then counted the rewards that we had been searching for, these were the special pop bottles that Mr Harrison at the 'pop shop', as the lemonade factory was known, would give a halfpenny or penny for according to their size. We had to wash the bottles in the beck – you got more for clean ones – and looking back I wondered if we even bothered to wash ourselves, I should say probably not.

Then we would take the bottles back and sometimes we had one shilling, sixpence, or more to spend on sweets and chocolate. I have always had a weakness for good chocolate, now you know where I get it from.

I started school at six years old at Addingham High Council School, being a late starter due to having been such an ill child in my early years. My first teacher was a kind lady; I got on with her and she taught me a great deal.

Just below mum's shop was a small greengrocer's shop owned and run by two sisters and their brother; it has since been pulled down but would have been about 80 Main Street. The two ladies were named Lotty and Lettie and they wore long black clothes down to their ankles. Their brother was called Tom and he delivered the groceries all over Addingham, Beamsley and Bolton Abbey on his cart, pulled by his faithful old horse Polly.

Now a few of us lads would play cricket across the Main Street by Whitakers Ironmongers, 72 Main Street, as the road was a shade wider there, and with a car or bus only every now and then, it made a good cricket pitch.

When the first school bell went at five to nine, we had to abandon the match and run or cycle to school up Chapel Lane and be in school for 9 o'clock. This we could manage each day with ease. Then one morning, as I was racing down the causeway to school on my bike, old Tom came out of the shop door with a box of apples in his arms. I caught the box with my shoulder but could not stop to see what had happened. The lads following behind said the full box of apples were all down the Main Street, some almost down to the Swan Hotel.

They told me they thought Tom had not seen the culprit; I prayed also that he had not. To the lads' credit, the headmaster at school, Mr Lemon, did not get wind of it, as he was a man who ruled the school with a rod of iron. I would have been in more trouble if he had found out.

I had my last two years in that school with this headmaster and hated every minute of it, as I thought, and still do, he showed a total lack of tact and encouragement to poor lads when they needed it. He also gave some very poor advice when I was a grown man, some that I did not ask for. But I got my own back some years later with a vengeance, I will explain more at a later stage.

While attending the school, which was next to John Cockshott's slaughter house, Mr Cockshott would shout over the wall into the school yard for six or eight strong lads to help with the killing of the beasts for meat. I was always one of the first over the wall. He required the beasts to be held steady while he performed the slaughtering. He would put a rope on the animal and pass this through an iron ring in the slaughter-house floor and then through a hole in the outer door, especially made for this purpose. We had to stand outside holding this rope steady until the killing operation had been performed. This always meant we were late into school and we missed some or all of one lesson. The headmaster never complained about our absence, which was very unusual indeed. We concluded that old John must have been giving him extra meat at the weekend.

Now Tom used to set off on his daily rounds with the greengroceries; his first stop would be just by the low end of the Swan Hotel. This was not far from 'Waffy' Horseman's barber's shop. Old Tom would stop Polly, his horse and cart, not that it was in anyone's way. Then the famous shout he was known for, 'owt you want', and all the women in the local houses would come out to buy.

But every time, before anyone had time to come out, 'Waffy' would come out of his shop and shout 'nowt you want', and then a screaming match would start between the two of them, but never more than shouting, this happened every single day.

Us lads used to love to hear the pair of them, before they finally stopped. Tom would then drive off down the road talking to the old horse, Polly, saying to the old mare, 'that so and so Waffy, that so and so Waffy', all the way down the village.

One day, while I was still in the room over the shop recovering from yet another illness, dad got very annoyed with some lads ringing the doorbell on the shop front door. He was a bit deaf but it sent mother and me mad. So he said he would teach these lads a lesson. He opened the window, which was directly above the shop door, and got a bucket of cold water ready for action in the bay window. It was of course a dark night and you could see nothing. He told me when that bell rang again, to say nothing, just nod at him and he would let those lads have the cold water.

Shortly after the bell rang, he let the full bucket of water go from the window. Below all we heard was a great scream, but it was a woman screaming and not the young lads.

Dad went downstairs to see to the lady, who happened to be one of his best customers! Do not ask me how he got out of that one; as for mum and me, we could not stop laughing.

At this time Uncle Fred and Aunt Eva lived in a small cottage, the end one on the row behind the old school and what is now the library, the cottage nearest to the old railway bridge. I often used to visit them in my very early years and on one of these visits, the unexpected happened.

Fred had always had a dog, usually a springer spaniel, but this day, as well as his own springer, he had this most lovely black cocker spaniel bitch pup, about three months old. I knew he bought and sold a few gundogs so it was no good me trying to beg it from him, but I did want this pup. So I thought that if I found out how much he would sell the pup for, I could go home and ask my dad if he would buy it for us. Remember I was only about six or seven at the time.

So I said to Uncle Fred how much will you sell the pup for? His answer was ten shillings. He had a smile on his face as he knew not one lad in Addingham would have ten shillings available for anything. But I had saved a few shillings and had more given to me for my birthday some weeks before and mum had changed them in the shop till for a ten shilling note.

I searched my pockets and found this screwed up ten-shilling note. I then produced it from my pocket and said, 'right, I'll have it, the pup is mine.' Fred's face turned from a smile to utter disbelief. Aunt Eva came to my rescue and said to Uncle Fred, 'you said ten shillings and he paid and the pup is now his and that's final.'

I was so proud walking home with the pup on a bit of string, it was a gem, and that is what we called her: 'Gem.'

He told people years later that if he had known I had ten shillings, the little so and so would not have got it. Dad trained this dog and she became one of the best gundogs around. So much so that grandad James at Pace Gate would borrow her for the grouse shooting season from 12 August to 10 December, then we would have her back at home until the following year.

Each spring, dad bred from her and she had a litter of about eight or so pups each year. I can remember them now: about four blacks, two blue roans, one chocolate and one black and white were the usual colours.

When she was two or maybe three years old she did something I have not known in any other dog. She went missing one July, then two days later we received a postcard from grandad James to say she had arrived at Pace Gate. Dad sent word back that he would collect her in December. Though before he could do so, one night in dark November, mum came home from one of the village drives she used to attend and fell over the dog which was waiting on the back door step to get in.

Pace Gate, 1935, author and Grandad James.

Dad gave the dog a good rub down as she was wet through. Now we realised she had travelled on her own via the shooting grounds she knew and swum the River Wharfe on both journeys. This dog did these trips every year for many years, the distance being six miles in each direction. It is wonderful how a dog can tell when it is July and then November.

The garden at our house and shop was at the back and had a stone wall right round it and three steps down to the gate. 'Gem' had her pups in the wood hut in this garden, and when the pups started running around dad used to leave the hut door open, so the pups could take exercise all day long. The old dog used to sit on top of the ash pit roof overlooking the garden. People and children could see the pups through the gate and loads of people used to admire them. Though if some of the more adventurous lads opened the gate to get a better view, the old dog was off the roof and down the steps like a lioness; the gate was then quickly closed.

At about this time mum said I should go to Sunday school. Being Church of England, I thought it was too far to go to St Peter's at the other end of Addingham. So I was sent to the Wesleyan chapel which was close to the high school I went to during the week. Much to my surprise I got to like the chapel Sunday school and the lady who took it. She told us many stories and many of the Holy Land and things about it. I did well at geography and nature studies at day school so I was thrilled to hear more about these foreign lands.

Then after a year or two a scheme came out at Sunday school whereby every time you attended you received a star on a card. At the end of every year if you got a full card you could receive one of the books on the Holy Land. I so wanted one of those books. I was never absent for one Sunday until about a fortnight before the presentation of the books. I fell ill with mumps, so I missed the last two stars on the card. These I should have been credited with anyway. When I returned, the books had been given out and there wasn't one left for me. I then thought that if that was the chapel's Christian outlook, it was not for me, and I never went again.

One day, while ill yet again and sitting in the bay window over the shop, it started to snow from the east, that being up the main street of the village. It started one Friday evening and continued non-stop until Sunday teatime. This became the great blizzard of 1933. Dad was working temporarily at the time as road watchman for Skipton Rural Council on Chelker road top. He operated the stop and go sign during the night as there were no traffic lights at this time.

Dad arrived home through the blizzard at about two in the morning and I heard him come into the house as I was obviously not sleeping soundly. I asked him why he was home at that time and his reply was that he was not stopping on Chelker any longer as not one vehicle had gone past him for the last five hours.

I watched all the men with horses and carts clear the main street and make a way through to Ilkley, taking the best part of a week. The road to Silsden needed about two weeks before vehicles and the bus service could get through. The road over Chelker to Skipton was blocked for seven weeks before being cleared.

One day in 1936, us lads heard that there was a big river and a flood in the fields around it. We set out to investigate this story, though we could hear the roar of the water before we got anywhere near the swing bridge.

One or two of us stayed to watch, the scene was really frightening but exciting at the same time. The river was up to the farm on the far bank and, looking at it today, this seems impossible but it was. The salmon ladders were in place then at the low mill and the river's water level was higher than it ever is now.

One man was halfway on the path from the farm to the bridge and struggling to make it, as he was then almost waist high in water. He did make it, and then somehow got over the bridge and to the steps at our side. We saw he was struggling up the steps and we gave him a hand up to the top.

He had his inside overcoat pockets full of rabbits. He had been poaching in the fields at Nessfield that had been flooded out by the high water level.

His name was Harry Hudson, and I was to work with him over thirty years later. He always said I helped to save him. But knowing his strength and determination, I think he would have made it without me.

Harry was the last man to cross that old bridge, because a few minutes later a huge tree came floating down the centre of the river at great speed. One great branch on the tree hit the middle of the bridge and the full power of it bent the bridge like a banana. This bridge was hung on two wire ropes, and when the tree hit the top rope upstream, it broke like a piece of elastic, then the second rope broke. The whole bridge and tree then went down the river together; it all took only a matter of minutes.

I should not think many people are alive today who witnessed this event.

The bridge was built in 1897 and this you can confirm in the book written on Addingham by the Civic Society. What the book does not say is the date of its opening. But there used to be a board on the bank on the Addingham side of the bridge that went downstream in another flood some years later.

That board stated that the date of opening of this first bridge was 18 July 1897.

It so happens this was my mother's birthday.

Now my final task I had to do was at Addingham High Council, though I did not know at the time that it was to be my last task. I had to sit an examination to see if I could pass to enter Ilkley Grammar School. We had to go to a school down Leeds Road in Ilkley for this examination and about twelve of us went this particular day. The examination consisted of a paper on maths (at which I hoped I was reasonable) and other papers on a variety of subjects. I thought at least I had not made a mess of things and would not be disgraced, though I thought others would have done better than me.

Before the results of these exams came through, mum and dad dropped the biggest surprise of my life so far: we were going to move to The Junction Hotel, Crosshills (now The Dalesway), owned by Massey's Burnley Brewery. Mum and dad had got the jobs of landlord and landlady. I had never even heard of the place.

MY LOST YOUTH

My lost youth started with the move to The Junction Hotel which was a very big shock to me. But an even bigger one came by post within a few days. I had passed my scholarship to Ilkley Grammar School and had to attend in a few weeks. My father promptly contacted the education authorities and told them I would have to leave home at 7.15 am, catch two buses to Ilkley and then walk for twenty minutes up to the school. Plus the same procedure in the evening, meaning I would be away from home for about twelve hours, and he did not think this was acceptable for a lad of eleven years. So he requested a transfer to Skipton Grammar School or Keighley Grammar School, both of which would be much easier to get to.

The education authorities would not even consider a transfer, and I was to go to Ilkley or not at all.

Dad would not let me travel that length of time and informed the authority I would not be going. Now, in Addingham High Council School, there is a large board with the names of all the scholars in gold letters, from the early 1900s, that have passed their scholarships. Some years later I saw that this board only contained the name of the lad who took my place when I could not go.

So I am sure I am the only person to have passed a scholarship at that school and never got his name on the board. So much for justice.

I was not at all happy at The Junction in my early years there, as I lost all my friends and was not one to mix and make new ones easily. So all my spare time was spent cycling to help on granddad's farm at Pace Gate, and I spent weeks and months there whenever I got the chance.

The highlight being at granddad's at Pace Gate in the middle of summer was the event known as the Midnight Walk. This was the best for us young boys and girls, who all came from the neighbouring farms to stay up after midnight to greet the walkers.

As far as I can remember, the walk started near Ilkley. I am not certain of the exact location, but the route went by Denton and then followed the wall that divides Beamsley Moor and Blubberhouses Moor, right over the moor top and finishing at Pace Gate.

Junction Hotel, Crosshills (now Dalesway), wartime,
note arms on road sign missing.

Our job was to help granddad keep all the lamps going which he placed on the small flat wall in front of the house. These were to act as a marker for the walkers to head toward when they came over the skyline. The job was not as easy as it sounds, as they were paraffin lamps and had to be pumped up all the time to give a good light. The wind, of course, kept blowing them out and you had to hurry into the stable and relight them. You had about six lamps going at the same time, and it was a laugh a minute to keep them all lit.

When the walkers' lamps, which they carried, came into sight over the skyline, a cheer went up from all the children. Grandmother would start to get the hot water ready to make tea. We all had a midnight feast. At times there could be up to thirty walkers and with all us children and adults, sometimes nearer fifty. My grandmother made all the food; sandwiches, cakes, everything homemade. She must have been paid for this, but I never saw any money changing hands.

The meal over, the walkers would go back over the moor to Ilkley and we were all allowed to stay up to see their lights disappear over the sky-line. Then everybody went to bed 'sharpish'.

Walking is again getting more popular, and I would love to see some of these old events rekindled.

Grandad had a lot of poultry, and I got a good knowledge of how to look after them, which was to come in handy for me when, years later, I myself started to keep first poultry and then pigeons, with which I had great success in later times.

The Junction was much larger than it is today: at the back were four other cottages, three garages and many stables and farm buildings. It had been a coaching inn and a farm many years before.

But I had to return to school for what was to be my last three years. Dad had by now arranged for me to go to the local school at Eastburn because the headmaster was a cricket fan, like my father, and he thought I would be happy there. I was pleased to go.

The Junction Hotel became a very popular pub and nearer the war years, when the Woodburn Café Dance Hall was in full swing, it was the place to be. But not for a lad of ten to fourteen who had to stay upstairs out of the public rooms all of the time. I was fed up with the place in general and vowed that I would never bring children up in a pub. Years later I had the chance to take over a pub, but I refused and must say I never regretted it.

I continued to play cricket at school and with any team that would give me a chance of a game.

My first recollection that I had some ability at the sport was in the school playground. We used to set the field placing's in the correct order: mid-off, mid-on, cover point, fine leg and so on. The headmaster must have been watching, unbeknown to us, because one day he came and asked the young lad fielding at cover point, 'Why is Holmes always batting at that end?' The lad replied, 'Sir, he is the only one who can hit a six over the road out of the school grounds, over those large trees and into Mrs Hattersley's orchard.'

I thought my career was at an end before it had even started. But the headmaster just smiled and went back into school.

Now, I would have been more fed up than I already was, but for one man who used the room above the stables to keep rabbits and pigeons. His name was Walt Horner, and although he was many years my senior, he treated me like a friend, and at that time I was really in need of one.

This man's skill at getting rabbits, pigeons and poultry ready for showing was outstanding, and I learnt a great deal from him which I put to my own advantage years later.

We had only one electric light and several oil lamps and we used to spend hours grooming the rabbits and making sure no white hairs were showing among the blacks hairs on the Dutch rabbits.

On one occasion, Walt left me to take two rabbits in a box to a show and I had to be at Kildwick station for this early time one Saturday morning as he was going to be at work and therefore had to rely on me.

On the morning when I arrived to put the two rabbits in the box, one of the rabbits I was to send had somehow got out of its cage and been fighting with another one that had done the same, and both had lost a lot of fur!!

So I did what I thought best and entered an older Dutch buck in its place. This one had been a good winner in the past, but Walt would not show it now as he said it had aged too much and he would use it for breeding, plus it had a few too many white hairs in the wrong places. I put it in the box and made it to the station just in time to catch the train.

When Walt came round at lunchtime, he thanked me for doing my best, but said our chances of winning had gone.

At night, I went to the station to collect the rabbits off a late train. When I got the box off the platform with my bike, which I could then ride home on, I had a quick look in the box to see if we had any prize card. I could not believe what I saw, we had about ten, all firsts: best Dutch, best adult, best of breed, best in show and many more. When I got back to Walt, who was waiting with the oil lamps on, ready to feed the rabbits, he could tell by my face that I knew we had won something. After opening the box and seeing the prize cards, he was utterly speechless. When he got his breath back, with a big grin on his face, all he said was, 'they must have been judged in a dark place'.

Later on, he started to race a few pigeons to an outbuilding next to the one in which he kept the rabbits. I really fancied pigeon racing after seeing them come back to The Junction and thought I would like to do that if ever I got the chance. One Friday morning, at 6 o'clock, I had to take three pigeons on my bike to Kildwick station for Walt, which I did. They were being sent by rail to Southampton and then by overnight boat to France to a place called Pont Le Veque. They were released on the Saturday morning and I clocked one bird in for him late Saturday afternoon. He won third prize in, I think, the Old Sutton Pigeon Club. I remember it was a blue hen; Walt missed it as he was at work.

When I tell some of the present-day pigeon fanciers that I sent birds on a Friday to France and had them home from the race on the Saturday, they do not believe me. But it was true and that was almost sixty years ago. Now the pigeons are sent by road, and have to set off on a

Wednesday or Thursday to get to France to race on Saturday; they call this PROGRESS!

As I stated before, my father died in 1942, but prior to this, the war had been on for three years and many men had been called up for the army. In 1941, Anderton's, which was on Keighley Road, Skipton, had a branch works of the Massey's Burnley Brewery which was of course the brewery that owned the hotel where we lived. The manager of Anderton's came to ask me and my father if he would let me go and work for him in Skipton; he was so short of men, with a lot of his employees away in the war. I said I would go for a fortnight to help him over the Christmas period. I stayed with the firm for over two years. In fact, I did enjoy the work and was glad to have some company away from The Junction.

In those days there were twenty-two pubs in Skipton, and I delivered beer, pop or wine to every single one. I thoroughly enjoyed the trips we had to make to Malham, Kettlewell, Buckden etc., with beer and pop in hay time, and many times we did not get back until late on Saturday afternoons. I loved the Dales then and I still do now.

In around 1940, I got a letter one day which was the surprise of my life so far. It was from the Yorkshire County Cricket Club inviting me to go for trials at the Ilkley ground for two days the following week. I do not know to this day who recommended me for these trials. The only person I still think it could have been was Mr Fletcher, my former headmaster. However, I arrived at Ilkley cricket ground and was met by several of the then Yorkshire cricket team. A few other young men were also at the ground and we played a two-day match, including a good few players from the Yorkshire team. I thought I had had a good match and batted well.

Just under two years later, I was called again by Yorkshire County Cricket Club to go once more to the Ilkley ground for a further two-day trial. This I did, and again, I thought I played a good match.

I am sorry to this day that nothing came my way from the trials, but the war was serious by then and the country was in a bad state with rationing of food, petrol and many other things. A lot of cricketers had gone to the war, including some of those who'd been at the trials.

I myself went unexpectedly to war in 1943 and was not to return to this country until 1947, by which time all chance of playing for Yorkshire had long gone.

During the early part of the war, the local council requisitioned one of the garages at The Junction to act as a mortuary for the area should the Germans drop bombs on Crosshills and district and cause casualties. This garage opened onto Skipton Road and so was out of site of a lot of other property.

I have in recent years asked many Crosshills people if they know where the old mortuary was and hardly anyone does. Inside the garage, the council men built up brick pillars with a six-foot or seven-foot block placed on top, but they made only thirteen places for any would-be bodies. I often wonder who at the council offices could arrange that only thirteen people could be killed at any one time.

In the early months of 1943, no one could be called up for the army until they had reached the age of nineteen. So, with a bit of luck the war could be over before I had to go. But this was not to be: the powers that be changed the rules in about the April of that year, and now anyone over the age of eighteen could be called up. Within a day or two of my birthday on 13 May, my papers arrived to call me up.

I had to report to Berwick-on-Tweed on 1 June 1943, when I was just eighteen years and a fortnight old. I became one of the youngest people to be called up at that time.

I said my farewells to all at The Junction Hotel and went on my own to Kildwick station as I did not want a fuss, but little was I to know that I would never again live at The Junction, or at home with my mother.

THE WAR YEARS

When I arrived at Berwick-on-Tweed station, many other young men also got off the same train, and we were met by trucks and regular soldiers who took us to our barracks, just north of the town.

We were then shown to a room containing about twenty single beds and were told this was to be our home for the next six weeks, by which time we would be trained in the use of army equipment and then sent to a unit or regiment for the rest of the war.

The beds had three hard pieces of sponge covered in dark, rough material, about a yard square. You placed all three on the bed in a straight line to form a mattress; they called these square things biscuits. They could not have been further removed from a biscuit. You then covered the self-made mattress with the two grey blankets and this was to be your bed.

Next, we collected all of our clothing and equipment and then a rifle. They gave us NO bullets for the rifles, which was a good thing, as many had never seen a gun. I had seen dad with his gun many times and I had shot a rabbit or two on my granddad's farm, so I knew how to handle a gun. I am sure many of the young men would have shot each other before the day was out if they had received proper bullets.

Next came teatime on this, my first day in the army. We had to form a long queue when going past this long table. We all received a knife, fork and spoon, a tin mug and a tin plate. Then continued on to collect our food: first, two slices of white bread, then somehow I missed the piece of butter, but you could not turn back if you missed anything; next a pot filled your mug with something they called tea. I had seen better peat water flowing down the River Wharfe. Lastly, on with your tin plate and on which you got a spoonful of red jam, and then, finally, they put on the same plate a fine kipper!!

I did not think life and food could get any worse than this, but almost a year later, it did.

Apart from all the army training, we also played many sports to get all the lads fit. I took part in many of the events and won the final of the 100-yard sprint out of the people that took part from all the camps on Berwick-on-Tweed. I beat a lad from Bradford Grammar School who thought he was unbeatable. I won by about two yards, the time was about 10.4 seconds which is still pretty good sprinting even today.

Now, the next event that made a world of difference to my life in the army happened while I was playing on the wing in a rugby match. I got my right leg twisted in a hole in the ground and my knee swelled to twice its normal size. I had all the normal checks; nothing was broken but the swelling would not go down, and did not do so for many weeks.

I was graded A1 when I joined the army, but if anything happened to you during your service, you had to be re-graded.

The grades, as I remember them, were about A1 to A4, B1 to B7 and C1 to C3. Whoever could make sense of that lot, I do not know.

However, I was sent from Berwick-on-Tweed to Edinburgh Castle by rail to be re-graded. After getting off the train at Waverley Station I had to walk all the way up to the castle.

My leg when I got to the castle was enormous, and I was re-graded B7. I wished many times I had gone up on two sticks, then I might have got a C grade and that would have been my discharge from the army. But you do not do those things at only 18.

After completing the six weeks training at Berwick, we all had to parade to be told which place we would be moving to the next day.

A sergeant then read from a list the names and places we were to go to. People had to go all over England but in the end only three of us were still waiting. He then said, 'you three are going in the Royal Army Medical Corp at Beckets Park Hospital in Leeds. Hand in your rifles, you are not allowed these in the medical corp.' Then he looked at the list again, 'I do not believe this,' he said, 'the best three shots with a rifle going into the medical corps, no wonder this war has lasted four years.' He then gave me my army no., 14647572, and never forget it!!

I served my medical training for six weeks in Leeds at this hospital. I had at least a knowledge of sorts because I'd been gutting rabbits for years and knew the names and locations of rabbits' organs; the human body is not a great deal different. Then I got posted to various hospitals, no doubt to give me extra experience. Just some of the ones I worked at were hospitals in Oswestry, Basingstoke, one in Abbeyfield Road, Sheffield and Conaught Hospital, Woking, to name just a few.

Each time, between hospital postings, I had to return to the RAMC base depot at Crookham in Hampshire. The nearest station to this place was Fleet in Hampshire, a three-mile walk away. Going to and leaving this place many times, I got to know every inch of this road.

We have now got to the early spring of 1944 and it is fairly common knowledge in the base camp that we were about to invade France.

Then, one evening, about 20 of us were instructed to catch a special train at a certain time for an unknown destination. We all thought this was the invasion of France about to start.

When the train arrived it was very full of troops, but we all got on board and away we went. I noticed it had two large engines on the front, so I thought maybe we were going further than the south coast. It was now very dark and you could see nothing from the windows of the train, plus all the lights in England were out with the blackout. When passing through a station you could not tell where you were, as all the names had been removed.

After being on the train about four hours I knew we must be travelling north, so I started to look at the hillsides in the moonlight and could now tell we were heading into Yorkshire. At last I recognised the landscape in the dark: just coming into Keighley. We then came up the Aire Valley past Steeton, then Kildwick, my home being only half a mile away, but at this time I did not know I would never return there!!!

I told most of the lads the stations further up the line, including the now-famous Settle to Carlisle railway. Next morning, we arrived at our destination: Greenock, on the Clyde.

We boarded the liner 'Orantes', a 30,000-ton liner that had been converted into a troopship.

The following evening, under cover of darkness, we sailed down the Clyde past Dunoon and out to the open sea.

Next day, I realised we were not going anywhere near France, as the sun was now shining and I could tell by its position that we were sailing due west. I thought we could be going to the Far East where the war with Japan was still at its worst, and thought we could be going to that theatre of war via America.

We sailed west in convoy for two days, surrounded by destroyers and other warships. On this day the German U-boats tried to attack the ships but many depth charges were dropped by the warships; by now, however, the sea was getting rough and we could see very little.

During the night a force nine gale hit the convoy and even the front of our 30,000-ton ship was even pitching into the sea. We had 24 men to a mess deck of about 10' x 20' with a table down the middle. This mess deck roof had 48 hooks in it; two hooks each for your hammock. You had to put this up and sleep in it, taking care not to fall out.

On this day we had only 18 men for breakfast, five for dinner, and I failed to get to tea due to being very seasick indeed and ready to die!!

We had a little battery wireless and had it tuned to a English station, and the horse race being broadcast. It could have been a wartime classic, even the Derby, which itself was never run on the normal race course at Epsom as this was not in use. However, the horse that won was called

'Ocean Swell'.

I think the rough weather saved us from further attack.

Over the next two days we sailed due south, then the next two due east.

Remembering my geography at school, I knew we were heading for the Strait of Gibraltar and into the Mediterranean.

The following morning we sailed past Gibraltar and the sun was shining on the large rock, and it was one of the finest sights I have ever seen. We then followed the coastline to keep out of the range of enemy bombers; then one night, under cover of darkness, we sailed into the Grand Harbour at Valletta in Malta.

This island had just been awarded the George Cross for holding out so long against the bombing of the Italians and Germans. You could see from the docks that the place was in near ruin.

We were to sail again the following night after not even being able to go ashore, only to go as far as Sicily, which had already been captured.

Our troops were fighting their way up Italy when we heard the invasion of France had taken place.

The RAMC started the 33 General Hospital in Syracuse in Sicily, and as our troops moved further up Italy, we moved up as well. First to Catania, then Taormina, then on to the mainland of Italy. We continued north until we finally came to a small place called Nola, just east of Naples.

All this time we had been treating hundreds of wounded soldiers as we were equipped to deal with 1500 patients at any one time. Since one night I know we had 3001 men in hospital, you can see we had no more facilities left to treat anyone else.

Just before we arrived up to Nola to take over this hospital, our food ration was late to arrive, and we lived on bread, bacon fat in tins from America (their pigs must not produce any lean meat, just fat) and MEL-ONS. It was about a month before we got our rations back to normal.

But I have never eaten MELONS since!!

Then a Canadian hospital team came to take over from us, and we boarded a ship in Naples and we were on our way home.

I reported on arrival in England, back again to the RAMC depot at Crookham, but I was only there for about two weeks when I was posted yet again. This time to the British Medical Hospital in Haifa, Palestine.

It was still early in 1945 and though we appeared to be winning the war in Europe, the war in the Middle East was still raging.

I sailed once again into the Med but this time from Southampton and arrived some weeks later in Port Said in Egypt. I had to stay in a place called Ismailia, waiting for transport to cross the Suez Canal. Whilst waiting, we had one day with a severe sand storm, this place being in the desert. The sand was everywhere: in your socks, shoes, bed, hair, up your nose and in your ears. If there is a place I would say not ever to visit, this is it.

Then I got word transport was available to cross the canal and a train forward to Haifa.

On the day of crossing the canal in a flat-bottomed boat, it started to take in water, and I said aloud, 'This is going to sink!' The reply I got from the driver of the boat was, 'It will not BOB.' It was an old friend from Primary School, Cecil Ellen, driving. What a small world!!

I finished my journey to Haifa by rail, in a cattle truck. But it was all worthwhile because I had the best two and a half years in the army in Haifa.

Upon arrival in Haifa I was promoted to Corporal to take charge of the admissions of all the patients into hospital, all accidents and emergency cases. I had staff on duty 24 hours a day and no one got turned away.

The hospital staff consisted of about 10 doctors under the leadership of Major Harold Park, a Harley Street surgeon, and about 50 RAMC staff under the control of Sergeant Major, a regular soldier. Then about 20

Queen Alexandra's Royal Nursing sisters, each of these given the rank Lieutenant because they were on war service.

Author, aged 19, Sicily.

Some of these, including Jalama, Nazareth, Bethlehem, Jerusalem, were places I had heard all about in Sunday school. What a shock I got, I had never seen such dirty places before and I now know that whoever had written these lovely stories of the Holy Land had never actually seen the places.

I had my twenty-first birthday in Haifa, but I was on duty that day, so

I did not tell anyone and no one ever knew.

Shortly after this, I fell over a loose threshold coming into the barrack room, so three of the lads carried me to the X-ray room to photo my ankle to see if anything was broken.

I was sat on the X-ray table while the X-ray lad developed the film. I knew by his face and the pain in my ankle that it was broken. I said let me look at the slide and when he did so, the door opened and in walked Major Park, the man in charge of the hospital. He must have seen the light on under the door. Now we're in trouble, I thought, because we should not have been there. He was dressed in his best uniform ready for going out!!

'What is going on?' he said when he saw it was some of his own RAMC staff.

I was the one on the X-ray table holding the plate, so I said, 'I have broken my fibula.'

He took the plate from me and I was expecting to be in trouble when he again said, 'So you have.'

He then turned to a lad called Ernest Harper, who was one of the three lads, and who happened to be Major Park's own operating assistant, to go get the things for a plaster cast, and he rolled up his sleeves and put me a cast on while I still sat on the X-ray table.

I got a rocker on the base of the cast the next day and went to duty in the reception by lunchtime.

Many of the hospital staff remarked next day, how did you get that cast on during the night. I replied that Major Park did it for me in person. They did not believe me!!

Now, we had different doctors on duty with us in the accident department each day, and some would do a lot of the jobs and some would say put a few stitches in a wound. I did a great amount of this type of work, but you always remember the very first time you have to put stitches in someone.

My first time was over a year earlier, in Catania in Sicily, and just my luck, it had to be a girl. She was a WAAF who was stationed at the airport in Catania, and had split open the top of her head when getting out of a truck. It required two stitches.

She was a young, dark-haired girl of about my own age of 19. I said to her I shall have to cut a small amount of hair from the wound to stitch it. She then started to weep a bit, so I told her I would not make a mess of her hair. After I had finished she thanked me and said I had not hurt her; little did she know how shaky I had been. But this remark did go some way to restore my confidence.

Now, as I remarked before, no guns of any kind are allowed in a military hospital by the terms of the Geneva Convention, agreed at the end of the First World War in 1918.

One day in Haifa, a Black Watch Captain came to the desk in reception with a bad cut on his left hand. I noticed he had a large revolver on his side.

I said to him that I would get the doctor to see his hand in a minute or two, but would he please hand in his revolver to the armoury next door. His remark to me was, 'My revolver never leaves my side. Get me a DOCTOR!!!'

I went in alone to see the doctor on duty, who happened to be Major Park himself.

I explained the situation to him but really he was a surgeon not a military man. I said he is only a Captain and you are a Major and he will have to do as you say, but he will take no notice of me as a Corporal.

So the Major put on his jacket, with his crown on the lapel denoting a Major, because he always worked in a cool shirt. He then went out into the reception and looked at the Captain and said, 'Has my Corporal told you about that revolver?' At the same time, he looked at his injured left hand and said, 'If that hand is not treated today you could have gangrene setting in by tomorrow.' I never saw anyone get to the armoury door as fast.

One day, while talking to Major Park when he was on duty with me as the Duty Medical Officer, I asked him who was looking after his practice in Harley Street while he was abroad with the war, or had he closed the practice for the duration of the war.

He replied that all at home was the same as his wife was a surgeon and was keeping the practice open while he was away.

I then remarked that should his wife ever require surgery he could operate on her, and she could operate on him if required, at least both free of charge.

To which he replied, 'Yes I could operate on her if I had to', then slowly added, 'But I would not have her within a mile of me with a knife!!' From that moment, I decided I would not ever pay Harley Street prices if ever I could afford to do so, as you never know who is holding the knife!!

At this time, an old Arab man used to come round the hospital selling grapes to the patients.

He had only a barrow type of cart, and on the front had about six bunches of the finest black grapes you had ever seen. But he was a smart cheat, and he was quick, so that after he had gone and you looked at your grapes they were some terrible ones he had put in your bag.

But one day he did it once too often, and the lads in reception waited for him. They then pelted him with these sad grapes all the way down to the gates.

We got no more bad ones!! They should not have done that, as his PRICE was only 6d a KILO!!!

Another event that pulled me up very sharply was when two men from the Engineers' Regiment came to the desk and put a large brown parcel on the front of it.

I was just about to tell them what to do with the parcel being stuck in the way, but I thought just in the nick of time that something was unusual.

So I said, 'What is that?'

One of them replied, 'That, my friend, is all that remains of the Pilot Officer who crashed that plane behind Mount Carmel last night.'

My reply, 'Then would you kindly take the parcel two doors up the corridor to the mortuary, we only have them here that are still living.'

We are now to about the middle of 1946 and the war is over all round the world, and soldiers are waiting to be demobilised (demob to us all!).

This system of demob was based on two things: age plus length of service. The number you received was based on these two factors; the lower your number the sooner you got home. I did not think the system very fair, because someone aged 28 who had served a year or so in England would be home long before someone like me aged 21 yet who had been on active service in a war zone over three years.

However, that was the arrangement and I was in group No. 55.

About this time, if you had been on active service overseas you could apply for a month's leave at home if you had served over two and a half years; mine was granted.

About this time I was made up to Sergeant, but I told the Sergeant Major that I did not want promotion, because it was well known that Sergeants were not being demobbed, so as to train the new recruits. He said I will not put your promotion through to England so you will get demobbed as a Corporal, but here in Haifa you are a Sergeant and will get paid as that.

His father and mother had an hotel in Lancaster, and he knew my parents had been in the same trade, so he had a thing in common with me.

Six of us, including Ernest Harper and myself, set off from Haifa to come home for this month's leave. With us a dark-skinned Arab from the Sudan. He was a good friend to us all, having been at the hospital over three years. They called him 'Shmandi' and he was employed by the British to clean the hospital and was paid a good amount by the government.

He was older than any of us and sort of looked after us, and would buy us things from the Arab market at the right price. We always gave him some money for doing this for us.

One the way down by train to Port Said, he would show us a photo of his little boy of about 5, but would not show us one of his wife.

He had finished work for the army and was on his way home to the Sudan.

Arriving in Port Said, we all had to go to the docks to get a boat home: he was getting a train to Cairo, then on home.

We all teased him about his wealth: he had more money saved than all the six of us had put together.

After saying our last goodbyes at the station, one of the lads said, 'Now Shmandi, tell us what you are going to do with that money?'

'Seeing as I will not see any of you again, I will tell you,' and without a smile and being very serious, he said, 'I am going home to buy another WIFE.'

We all laughed and he could not understand why; he wanted two wives and we hadn't one between the six of us!!

When we got on the ship coming home, Ernest Harper said we are not going down in a mess room on this trip, come with me and we will find the ship's doctor.

When he found the ship's doctor he informed him he was Major Harold Park's operating room assistant and would he like any help on the trip home.

He knew of Harold Park because he wrote for the 'British Medical Journal' even when in Haifa. The title of his articles were always 'Interesting Operations I Have Performed' by Harold Park.

So the doctor was glad to have our assistance and we slept in the ship's MI room on the stretchers, and we had a grand trip home.

On arrival home I went to see Uncle Jim and Auntie May, to whom he had got married in the early part of the war. They were now farming at Pace Gate. I also paid a visit to Swinton to see mum and my new stepfather, but Swinton was not my cup of tea, so I came back to Uncle Fred and Aunt Eva and stayed with them until I returned once again to the depot at Crookham.

I was to see Ernest back at Crookham but he never returned to my knowledge, so I have never known what happened to him.

The demob numbers had now got to about 50 or 51, so I expected it to only be a week or two before it was to be my turn.

On returning to the depot I reported next day to the company office, and was told to see a certain young officer. On finding him in his office he asked me my usual particulars. I then told him I was due for demob in a week or two.

He said 'Where's your demob book?' I told him I had never seen a demob book and hadn't any idea of what one looked like.

He then said, 'Where's your unit?' My reply was 'Haifa, Palestine.'

Then, to my great shock, he said, 'Well you'll have to go back to your unit and fetch it!!'

So next morning I went to the RTO (that's the travel arrangers) and received a travel warrant and I was then on my way back to Haifa.

Just before setting off again for Southampton to get a ship, I met a pal called Alex Bovington who had been with me in Italy in the thick of the war. He was dressed in his best uniform with all his medal ribbons on and he had many of these, being a regular soldier, and he'd served in India before the war.

I asked, 'What are you doing here?' His reply, 'NOTHING.'

He then explained that the five companies in the depot were A, B, C, D and E. He was carrying a few books under one arm and if any officer or NCO asked him what he was doing, if in A company he said he was D company runner, if in E company, he was runner for B company, and so on. He said I have been here over six weeks Bob and they haven't found me yet!

It took me six weeks to get back to Haifa, and I went up to the company office in the hospital, but all the nurses and many men I knew had gone, so on entering the office, who should be coming out but my old Sergeant Major.

He was very shocked to see me, and said, 'What have you arrived back here for Bob?!'

I explained about the demob book, and what he said about that young officer is unprintable here.

He then marched into the office and found my demob book in the bottom drawer, and then said, 'Right Bob, you can go home now!!' I had been travelling for six weeks, so I asked if I could stay the night and go tomorrow as I could do with a wash and clean up.

'By all means' was his reply, 'there is a spare room in the Sergeant's mess, take that for the night and meet me in the mess for dinner tonight.' He looked at my Corporal stripes that I had put back on to come to England and said, 'never mind those, you are still a Sergeant in Haifa.'

Next morning, I set off back down the old railway to Port Said. On arriving there I waited about three weeks for a ship home; they were all coming up the Suez Canal full of troops from India, Burma and the Far East and not one would take anymore.

Then we heard that if we went up to the port of Alexandria we may get a smaller ship going to some port in Europe.

We stayed only a couple of days before we got an old banana boat going across the Med to the port of Marseille in France.

Just three of us got on this boat and it was so slow we seemed to be ages before we got to France.

Then we came through France by rail. None of us could speak a word of French, but after overcoming a great deal of confusion in Lyon (we kept asking for Lions!!) we made it to the port of Calais.

We crossed the Channel by ferry and were then making our way to the demob centre in York.

But the last bit of disaster came when we were rushing on the underground in London to catch the train. On the escalator at Leicester Square, we were changing trains to King's Cross when one of the lads lost his kitbag from his shoulder. The escalator was crowded and the kitbag bounced on everybody's head to the bottom. When he got to the bottom, he picked it up and carried on as if nothing had happened!

At York, there was not a great deal of clothing left to pick from now, because too many troops had been before me. I got the usual shoes, brown suit, a mac – you kept what underclothes you had with you – and a couple of shirts that matched none of the other things. I told the chap in charge I did not want a hat, I said I would not wear another and I never have!!

On the way from York to Addingham via Leeds, I wondered what the future would hold for me!!

I reviewed my position:

My father had been dead years

My mum had remarried and gone away NO permanent home

NO trade NO job.

ONLY the clothes I had with me and £75 for four years away.

My position had to improve from this state, and I am glad to say it did, very quickly.

I arrived home to Addingham to Fred and Eva's in about April 1947, and I had missed the big snow of that year, but I had seen many places in the world, although many of the things I saw I could have done without. And I was not yet 22 years of age.

A HAPPY YEAR AT THE CROWN

I arrived back to the Crown Hotel in Addingham, where Fred and Eva made me so welcome. She had got the little bedroom over the snug ready for me if I should wish to stay. She said they would like me to stay and help them in the pub as it was getting a bit too much for her, but Fred would not retire. Eva said if I helped them both I need not pay any board.

With this arrangement settled, I was delighted, but the next move Eva made was to take most of my £75 and open an account for me in Martins Bank across the road from the Crown.

Now, these were happy times with all the young men and women returned home from the war, and it was a time for parties and dances, even though meat, butter and things were still rationed and clothing coupons were like gold. It was no good having money for clothes if you had no coupons.

Dancing had gone on for most of the war years in Addingham at the low school and at the Crown. The one at the Crown was held outside in an old clubroom over the stables, where the old railway horse was stabled. These dances were to records of waltzes, foxtrots, quick steps, barn dances and so on.

When the music and noise got too loud, the old horse would play up in the stable below, kicking and so on. We had to stop until he was alright then carry on.

The dances were organised by two men called Charlie Ducket and Albert Whitaker.

These two had very little money to spare, as had many others, but during the week would stand at the Crown bar drinking the cheapest drink possible half-pint of mild beer.

The dance was held in aid of the Forces, or at least it was supposed to be, but on dance night you could find them at the Crown bar drinking

Guinness and a tot or two of whisky.

Someone must have thought the profit was not right, because when they put a large board outside the Crown saying:

MR. C. DUCKETS GREAT EFFORT FOR THE FORCES

During the night it was changed to: THE FORCES

GREAT EFFORT

FOR MR. C. DUCKET!!

About this time four lads, who I will not name now, went in a small car to Silsden for a drink.

Coming home, at the corner by the Old Bar House, a sheep walked into the road and they hit it and killed it. The sheep was put into the boot of the car, taken behind the Sailor, gutted, skinned and cut in four, and mutton was on the menu at the weekend!!

Another man called Harry Wood from Bolton Abbey used to come to the Crown every night for a drink or two, as it was then one of the most popular pubs in the district. He was on his old motorbike and sidecar, a Sunbeam I recall; what would that be worth today?! One night, after leaving the Crown, someone shouted that he had crashed on the Catholic church corner just down the road. We (the young men) ran down to the corner to see what we could do. The bike was on its side, so we put it back the right way up on the road. Harry got on again, kick-started it up and left in a cloud of smoke again for Bolton Abbey.

When he came into the pub the next evening, one of the locals who had not seen the event said to him, 'Harry were you drunk last night?'

Harry replied 'Of course not, I only had a gallon and a half of old beer!!'

At this time, Fred had just taken the shooting rights on Farfield Farm and paid £10 per year for this, which appeared to be dear at the time.

He knew what he was doing and for me it turned into a brilliant investment. This farm was about 350 acres, but it had another 1000 acres of good shooting ground around it. Remember, Fred had been the perfect poacher 30 years earlier. So my job was to drive all the game off the 1000 acres early in the morning onto ours, before we started getting the game on ours during the day.

Tommy Sutcliffe used to come to the Crown a lot at this time, and he was a gentleman with a good job. He was in charge of the wool control during and after the war and bought all the wool into England from all over the world. But he liked Wharfedale and we let him be partner in the shoot. So it was Fred, Tommy and myself.

One day, Tommy rang Fred and said could I go out and get him a brace of pheasants. It was like asking for gold.

However, at this time, and during the war, all farmers had to do some compulsory ploughing to grow food for the country. So, I knew of one field towards Bolton Abbey that was still ploughed and growing potatoes. I took Fred's springer spaniel Bounce with me. He flushed two pheasants from this field and I shot them both: a cock and a hen.

So when Tommy arrived at the Crown that night we had the perfect brace of pheasants.

He was so pleased when Fred told him I had got them for him. He said to me, 'I will bring you a good dog for doing that.'

A few days later, he arrived again, this time with the dog. It was a golden cocker spaniel pup, about six months old: the finest dog I had ever seen. It was registered at Crufts by the name of Grand Marnier of Berradale. I think that was the correct spelling, but we called him Chris.

Fred and I trained him over the next year because he had been brought up by a lady in Bradford and had never seen a green field or a rabbit in his life. He turned out to be one of the greatest gundogs that ever lived!

We of course still had Fred's dog Bounce, and he also helped to train him.

Bounce had a character of his own and we never had to shut him up at night; Fred sent him out of the kitchen door at bedtime with the words 'Go to bed!'. He would go straight into the stable and sleep with the railway horse. The door was always open for the fresh air, but if you looked out of your bedroom window first thing in a morning, he would be walking round Addingham as though he owned the place.

Now, about this time, a man called Alf Thompson lived just down Bolton Road from the Crown. He came in the Crown one day complaining that someone was stealing his milk. He was a big man, and said he would murder them if he found out who it was.

Milk was then delivered in a large milk churn, and you just put a basin outside and a saucer on top to keep out the dust.

A few mornings later, I was up just before Aunt Eva came downstairs. I said to her, 'I am going upstairs to see Fred,' which I did. He was still half asleep so I made sure he was awake and told him to get up and go and see Alf Thompson before he went to work. I had found out who was stealing his milk; it was his dog, Bounce. Not only had he drunk the milk every morning, today he had brought the basin home and it was on our kitchen step, still intact!!

However, I continued rabbit catching over the next two years, every possible way Fred taught me: netting, snaring, ferreting and shooting. As rabbits were selling at 7s/6d per couple, owing to the meat shortage, I was now in the money. We caught hundreds of rabbits, and what we could not sell in the Crown we sent to Bradford market by rail in wicker hampers.

We had some great times, both Fred and I with these two dogs, but as usual, Fred had got yet another dog on trial, a chocolate-coloured cocker spaniel that was about 18 months old.

This day, we decided to try Park Wood near Nessfield and drive that down to see if we could get a pheasant. This chocolate dog I left with Fred at the bottom of the wood, where we hoped the pheasants would fly past, if I could flush any out.

I went round to the top and drove the wood down with Bounce and

Chris. I knew that if there was a pheasant in this wood it would come out for these two dogs.

About halfway down, the pair of them flushed out a cock pheasant and it flew just to the place where Fred was waiting. I heard two shots and then no more. When I got down to the place where I left him, he was sitting under the wall smoking his usual cigarette, a gold flake. You don't see many of these now!

He said to me that he was getting too old now, and thought he had missed the pheasant, but then he looked over the wall for this chocolate dog. Suddenly he said, 'Look Bob, that chocolate dog is bringing the pheasant up the field in his mouth, I must have hit it.'

I got up, looked over the wall and told him he had better look again because the dog was bringing one of Layfield's Rhode Island cock chickens!! He said never mind, we will have chicken for Sunday lunch! And we thoroughly enjoyed it!!

The next little job I got at the Crown was as the mortuary attendant for Addingham. One thing about this job is that you do not have to worry much about other applicants. There are never many, or none at all.

It was always good on one's CV; it will get you noticed.

However, to the job itself. At that time, any bodies found had to be taken to the nearest public building until identified. With the Crown being the nearest place to the river, and with most bodies coming from the river, the Crown was the obvious choice.

We had a small room up a few steps next to the stable, and this was to be the mortuary.

When informed by the police, I had to prepare a trestle table on which I had to put a white cotton sheet. This I got from Aunt Eva and she was kind enough to wash it for me after each body had been identified and removed by members of the deceased's family.

I had only to open up for the police with the body, and for identification next day.

When no bodies were in store, Chris, my dog, used to sleep in this room.

Now the beck was at the back of this room and there were always a few rats around. So Chris slept in the room just the same when the bodies were in residence. Chris hated rats and would worry one on sight, so the bodies always rested in peace.

I got paid per body, and at seven shillings and six pence a time I only wished more people had been suffering from depression and had gone into the Strid at Bolton Abbey. That's where all my bodies came from, and when they washed down the River Wharfe were pulled out at High Mill, by the weir.

One week, I had one body on the Monday, one Wednesday and one Friday. I was in the big money, 22 and six in a week! The following week, I had none. Fred then said to me, 'I think your business is going bust!!'

About this time, Mr Keith Douglas, the owner of Farfield Hall and the estate around it, used to come to the Crown several evenings a week for a quiet drink of 'Pink Gins' and a chat with Fred.

He gave Fred permission to shoot pheasants on his land called Rispill Wood, which was on the other side of the river to Farfield Hall and was on the hillside leading up to Beamsley Beacon.

There used to be big shooting parties at Farfield Hall many years before we did any shooting. At that time, a footbridge was built over the Addingham to Bolton Abbey road. The purpose of this was to allow the shooting party to cross the road with their dogs in safety and go down to the river, where a boat was available to get across the river to Rispill.

All the local people called this bridge the 'Wishing Bridge' but Mr Keith told us the correct name was the 'Cuckoo Bridge.'

Now just downstream from the place where the boat used to be, was a steep wood on the Addingham side of the river, and one day we decided to try this wood for a pheasant, as one or two would sometimes fly there from across the river.

As usual, Fred stationed himself at the bottom of the wood and I drove the wood down with the two dogs. I saw nothing at all as this is a steep and rough wood to walk through. Halfway down, I heard five shots and I then knew Fred could not fire five shots at the same bird.

On getting down to him I saw he had five geese that were now dead but floating down our side of the river.

Chris had all five out of the river to us very quickly. He was a very good swimmer and far quicker than Bounce, although he was not a bad swimmer for a spaniel of his size and age.

We then had a right look at these geese and I said to Fred these are not wild geese but half-tame Canada geese. His reply was, 'Does it matter, they all taste the same!!'

When we got home, Fred went round to see the butcher at the Co-op just down Bolton Road. The butcher said he would pluck them for us and sell them in the shop, for a share of the profit. Fred agreed this with him, although I do not think Fred would have mentioned Canada geese. This was on a Tuesday, and he sold the lot before Thursday night.

On Friday, the Ilkley Gazette was published and I read Fred this advert from the paper:

LOST Five Canada Geese Could be Langbar Area!!

Fred's reply to this was someone should have saved their advert money!!

In the early days of 1947, two men came to the Crown looking for me. When Aunt Eva informed me they were in the kitchen, I knew they had to be someone she knew.

On entering, one was Uncle Jim; he was her younger brother, and the man with him was a slight relation called Bert Ward.

Just for your information, Bert Ward was the father of a girl about my own age who had those big fancy goods shops in Skipton and now in that special shop in Gargrave, now under her name, Dorothy Ward.

Bert Ward had come to ask me if I would play cricket for Bolton Abbey. I had previously asked about a game at Addingham, but no one knew me as a cricketer at that time and I was told they had plenty of players.

So I informed Bert I would be delighted to play for them. He said I would be opening the batting with George Harrison, whom I knew well although he was much older than me and was a good cricketer, and also that he, Bert Ward, was the captain.

Bolton Abbey cricket pitch had had a direct hit with a bomb from a German plane, trying to hit the Low Mill at Addingham which was making carburettors for the war effort. Five or six bombs missed everything except the cricket pitch all ben down the far side of the river to Addingham.

On the night these bombs were dropped, I was on leave from the Crown for a day of two and all of Addingham's people were on the streets as it was at night.

I must have got used to it abroad as I slept through it all. The cricket pitch had been repaired and Bert Ward got his team together for the 1947 season. I played for them for the next five seasons, when I finished owing to work commitments. I played again in the 1960s with another fine side, but the 1947 side was the best with there being so many ex-league players available.

To give you some idea of the quality of this side, here is a list of the team, in batting order. Very few sides came to Bolton Abbey and won.

We had some great games at Bolton Abbey, and the meals at teatime put on by the ladies were out of this world, all organised by Mrs Roy Newall and her committee.

After the cricket season finished in 1947, Fred and I continued with the rabbit and game hunting, and just before we got to the end of the year we were catching rabbits for a Mr Pullan at a farm called Wards End at the top of Langbar, nearly onto Beamsley Moor.

We were sat under a wall having a breather for the dogs, when Fred said 'SIT' and when he said SIT the dogs SAT and dared not move.

I saw he was looking further up the wall side. Then I saw he was looking at something coming towards us down the side of the wall.

We had a ferret of our own called Barbara and she was always with us. I will tell you more about her later.

Author and George Harrison.
Opening the batting for Bolton Abbey at Blubberhouses, 1947.

This thing coming down the wall was white but from its movements I knew it was too erratic for a ferret. Fred then raised his gun and when this thing came within range he shot and killed it, first shot.

We got up and examined this thing and it was a white stoat. You can tell a stoat from a weasel because the stoat has the last two inches of its tail black. This white stoat had the black tail, so there could be no mistake.

Fred informed me that the last time he had shot a white stoat was over 30 years before when out with my father. He said to me, 'you'll be a long while before you see another.' To my regret, I never have, and I should have brought it home and had it stuffed, but at the time you don't think that way. He buried it in the wall bottom and so with it went another piece of history.

So now we get to the end of 1947, which I had started with nothing to my name. Though as things turned out I had done very well. I hadn't bothered about getting a job, but had much more money by not doing so.

All in all I had had the best year in my life and been very happy. Though I was not to know that 1948 was to be even better!!

Keith Douglas at Fairfield Hall.

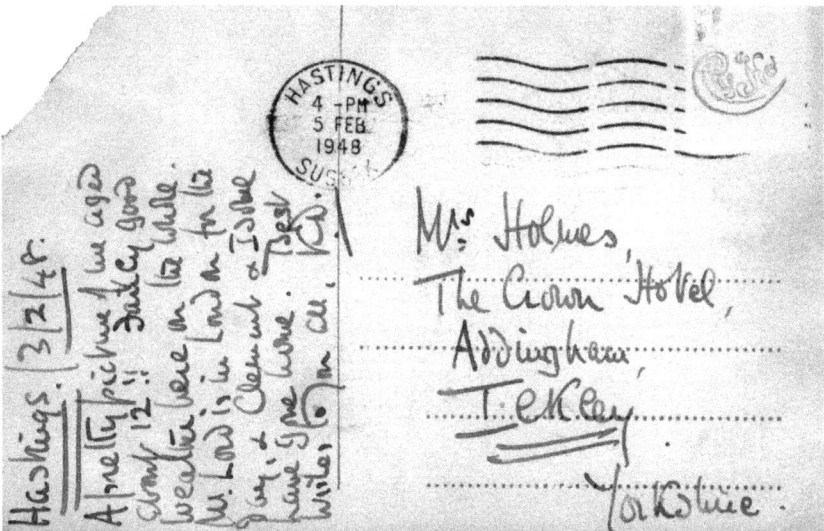

Postcard sent to The Crown from Keith Douglas after moving to Bexhill.

THE VINTAGE YEAR

In 1948, Keith Douglas, the owner of Farfield Hall at Addingham, decided to sell the hall and the surrounding estate. He was in poor health and was moving to Bexhill-on-Sea for health reasons.

I am sorry to record that this did not benefit him at all, as he died about one year later.

We had permission to shoot over the estate, and took a few brace of pheasant to the hall for Mr Keith each week. He liked pheasant, but was too ill to go with us and many times said he would give all his wealth away if only he could go with us.

The estate was from the edge of Beamsley Beacon down to the river and across the valley to the south and east of Chelker Reservoir.

The hall was sold prior to the estate, to the West Riding County Council for use as an old people's home. The rest of the 13 lots which comprised the estate were sold at auction for £26,465.

Today, that estate would be in excess of eight million pounds with all the farms and houses on it.

So the last of the great estates in Addingham came to an end.

We were still catching and selling a lot of rabbits in early 1948, the demand being very good. On one trip getting into late February or early March, rabbits must have been breeding early due to the mild weather. We had shot a few doe rabbits in milk which we never tried to do, however we had about six of these one day and we knew no local lads who would buy those kind.

A chap from Silsden called Ethelred Throup used to call in at the Crown yard with his horse and cart on his greengrocery round. Unknown to me, Fred sold him these six old rabbits full of milk. When he told me I said that he could see to him the following week as I was not going to deal with his complaints.

The following week, Ethelred arrived with his horse and cart on his round, as usual. So I sent Fred out to see him, and I stood back waiting for the complaints.

Fred said to him, 'Were those rabbits a bit milky last week, and did you sell them?'

His reply was, 'Yes, have you any more, they like bloody big ones in Silsden!!!'

Now one day, while hunting on the railway side one mile north of Addingham, we got caught poaching.

The railway at this point goes between two woods owned by the Duke of Devonshire. A lot of rabbits came out of these woods and onto the railway side.

We were keeping a lookout towards Addingham for the then railway inspector, who would prosecute on sight anyone on the line. Unknown to us, he came from the Bolton Abbey direction and we were caught without question.

We were sat on the banking giving our dogs a short rest, it was no good denying our position: two men, two dogs, one ferret box and 12 dead rabbits.

On seeing the inspector, Fred said to me, 'start eating your sandwiches'. When he got nearer he said to us, 'Now, now and what have we got here?'

Without replying to the question Fred said, 'Good morning Inspector.' Inspector: 'Oh! You know me.'

Fred replied without giving him the chance to say anymore. 'Yes, I see you pass quite regularly; you see, we're catching the rabbits in the two woods, they are damaging the young trees and it will be a long job, but I hope you do not mind us eating our sandwiches here before we go in the other wood, as the wood is full of flies and not very nice.'

The inspector replied, 'Not at all and while you're at it, catch them on the railway bank as well, or I could have problems with poachers!!!'

He walked off towards Addingham. I told you I was trained by an expert!!

One other event happened very shortly after this when we were just sitting inside a wood towards Bolton Abbey. It is often worth sitting quiet when hunting as you see game that you would not see if walking and charging about. After being sat still for a few minutes, we saw a man coming towards us from the direction of Addingham. We got further into the wood and out of his sight but keeping observation on him.

He then started to set snares, the time being about 4 o'clock and soon it would be getting dark. As far as we could see he set about 20 snares and then departed over the footpath back towards Addingham.

Fred then asked me if I'd noticed how far from the wall he had set the snares. 'Yes,' I said. 'Well then, you set off in the morning and be here for about half past four and collect all the rabbits from his catch and don't forget to collect the snares as well.' He said that will be before he comes at daybreak, and you will be able to see clearly because the moon is on the wane and it will be clear to see at that time.

I collected 10 or 12 rabbits and about 20 snares, and was home before half past five.

Even now, I wonder what the poacher thought when he got there about daybreak. Ever since, I have known the phases of the moon and many times turned it to my great advantage.

My daughter today says I am ruled by the moon! But just now she will not know if it's a new moon or on the wane.

Now, as I said before, the ferret was called Barbara, and was a white bitch ferret and had a two-compartment hut in the stable at the Crown. This was full of straw at one side and she used to eat at the other side. Ferrets are very clean animals and you do not touch or look in the breeding section when they have young, or they worry if they smell your finger near them.

Fred used to get her mated and have young in the spring. In the seven or so years she had young, she reared 49 young ferrets and never lost one.

We had the hutch locked so no one could look in at any time.

When the young were a few weeks old, they used to walk out of the sleeping compartment and into the other section, as they could hear Barbara eating. But if she saw you looking at them she would pick each youngster up in her mouth by the back of their head and take them back to bed, out of sight.

After a week or two, she would allow them to stay and eat with her; bread and milk at this stage. Later, when they were eating flesh, rabbits or rabbit liver, we would move the young ones only to a large hut in the yard in the fresh air. This was much larger than the breeding hutch, about three yards long by one yard wide, with a smaller sleeping compartment and a larger one for food.

Some years we had seven youngsters to move into this hut, and as they were untrained, would bite your fingers on sight. So you had to wear a thick glove.

Fred fed them every day on bread and milk and rabbit livers, but if a cat got killed on the road he would gut that as well, for they loved fresh blood. At night, they would look like a pack of lions covered in blood, but washed themselves every night and they would be clean again next morning.

This hut in the yard had a very large padlock on and we kept the key in the Crown. On the front of this hut was strong half-inch mesh to let in more air. One day, a young lad of about nine or ten was playing in the yard, from Bolton Road, and as his dad had a motorbike in one of the garages, I thought he was waiting for his dad. I had gone into the Crown when I heard a loud scream. On reaching the hut, I saw he had put a finger through the mesh on the ferret hut. One of the young ferrets had bitten through his finger with the six or so teeth they had at this age, and was in no way letting go.

I went into the Crown to get my thick glove and the key for the hut to get it off his finger. But by the time I got back he had tried to push another finger through the mesh to get it off, and now had four fingers and a thumb on one hand, all with a young ferret on each. When I had got them all off his hand one at a time, and when the last one was off, he went down Bolton Road faster than a rocket and did not return for years!!!

Now, when Fred closed the Crown at night, we would lock all the doors and Aunt Eva would clean all the tables, etc., and leave everything ready for the next morning. I would take all the empty bottles from the bar ready to take to the stores outside next day, and fill the bar with full ones in the morning.

Fred would then cash up by himself on the bar counter and under the counter he kept his daily account book. He never failed to keep his books up to date each day while it was still in his memory.

I followed this example years later when I went into business and found this to be the easy yet perfect way to keep accounts.

One night, though, he pushed an old coin across the bar to me and said, 'What is that?' I replied that it was an old worn silver three pence piece. Fred then said, 'look again more closely on both sides and read what it says.' The date was 1844, and on the same side, the letters FOUR. 'That bob is an old silver four pence piece, been out of circulation years,' was his reply.

He then said you may keep it, you may not see another. I have had this coin over 50 years now and many people have never seen one and I have yet to see another.

It will not be of any great value because it is so badly worn, but to me it is part of my family history and I hope in years to come my family will keep it for its sentimental value.

Inside the kitchen door at the Crown, hung on a hook, was Fred's catapult. He'd made this himself from a Y-shaped piece of hazelwood that would not snap, plus two lengths of square black elastic, joined together with a short piece of leather. On a shelf nearby were the lead bullets he had also made using a small hole in a buffet top, to get the required shape.

Now he hated cleaning up cat and dog mess in the Crown yard, and as the kitchen door was open most of the time, he could see anything coming into the yard.

If a cat should arrive in the yard and appear to be going to do its business on his property, Fred would quickly get his catapult down and one bullet would be all that was required. At the precise moment the cat got down to perform its bodily function, he would fire, not to kill or injure the cat, but to give it a rude reminder to go elsewhere!!

He was a good shot with a catapult, the best I have ever seen, and I never had to clean the Crown yard all the time that I lived there.

Now, a few weeks before the start of the cricket season, it was decided we would hold a dance in the school room at Beamsley. On this occasion, for some reason, James Harrison, my Uncle Jim, was not available, so as club treasurer, he said to me would I mind collecting the takings at the dance, take them home with me and let him have the money later.

I agreed and said it would be no trouble at all, as I was coming on my bike so could stay to the finish.

I got the money in my two jacket pockets, still my brown demob suit, after we had closed up at the dance, jumped on my bike and set off down Murk Hill towards Bolton Bridge. Now this hill was much steeper than it is today and you got a fast speed up even on a bike. On the left of this hill were many large trees, not now there, and the shadows from these trees made it very dark in certain places.

As I got full speed up in the middle of the hill, in front of me were two girls walking home to Beamsley, down the middle of the road on the white line. Everything then happened so quickly I had no chance to do anything. One girl moved to her right and the other to the left, so I decided to go between them. Both girls were wearing light-coloured dresses, so I thought it would be my only thing to do. That's when the crash took place. I never saw the girl between them in the black dress. I went clean over the handlebars and did not hit the road until I was almost at Beamsley Lane End.

When I sort of came round, I looked in my pockets and all the money from the dance was still there: I had gone over so fast nothing had fallen out; even my gold watch was still working. Mum and Aunt Eva bought that for me for my twenty-second birthday as I was away for my twenty-first.

My demob suit was still OK, so I stood up and walked slowly back up the road to see what had happened.

The three girls were from Beamsley, and I knew them all. The one in the black dress was out cold on the white line. So I sent one of the girls to the farm to ring for an ambulance and I said to the girl help me lift her sister onto the grass verge in case a car should come down the hill and they don't see her.

She had only one cut on her forehead, just on her hairline, so I knew when she got alright again she would have no major scars. I lifted her in my arms to the side of the road: she would only be about eight or nine stone, but as I was slowly putting her down on the grass verge my right shoulder – clavicle – snapped in two and the poor girl dropped the last few inches to the ground.

The ambulance soon arrived and we both went to Skipton General Hospital. She was kept in hospital for a few days and I was sent back home to the Crown by ambulance with my arm in a sling, but not before I told the nurse on duty to put the arm in a sling that was hanging down, not the blasted one I was using!!

It took me a few weeks before I could use my arm again. I had no further treatment and it healed on its own. Today it would have been wired,
but this was 50 years ago and too late now.

The girl and I remained friends until she left the area some years later.
Now the cricket season was about to start again, and my arm was out of
the sling, but not strong enough to hold a cricket bat and hit a hard ball.
So for the first two games I went along and watched the other lads play.

On the third Saturday I went again to watch, when Bert Ward said,
'You will have to play Bob, we're a man short.' 'Alright', I said, 'I will field
for you but I will not be able to bat.' He said I wouldn't be required to bat,
as we were fielding first and should get the other side out for a low score.

This they did for about 150 runs, so the Bolton Abbey side should have
scored these easily.

We seemed to be doing this very well, although our batsmen kept
getting out. At last, the score was 145 to us, requiring just 5 to win, when
another of our batsmen was out. That just left Nos. 9, 10 and 11 (me) still
to go in. Uncle Jim was doing well, 40 some not out, so if he could get the
strike we should be alright to win.

However, No. 9 was out first ball off the next over for a 'duck'. No. 10
was going in to bat when Bert said to me, 'get your pads on, you may have
to go in for a ball or so.' No.10 was then out first ball for a 'duck'. I was No.
11, so I went in with four balls still to face.

Jim came to meet me; he knew my situation, so he said run one off
the first ball you receive, so I can get to that end. I said OK as I knew I
would not last the remaining four balls with only my left hand being any
good. I then got ready for my first ball. I held the bat in both hands and
just took my right hand away from the bat handle at the moment before
the ball hit the bat.

It flew off the bat to a man fielding at backward point and I thought
we would never make the run, but he fumbled the ball and it went behind

him.

Now, as I am a right-handed batsman, you always run with the bat in the right hand, but on this occasion I could not do so. I grabbed the bat in my left hand and set off to run, but I did not see Jim running towards me very fast, as he was going to the danger end, and I hit him with the bat handle, but he still got to the other end. Looking back, I knew we had made one run but Jim was on his knees holding his head; I had hit him under his chin and he looked like passing out.

The other team wanted to take him off the field as this would have given them the win. At this moment, though, Bert Ward had seen the situation and was to us in a flash with a large jug of water. He saw Jim had his shirt open four buttons at the top. He always had his shirt open in any weather; they bred them tough on Blubberhouses Moor. Bert then held Jim's shirt open further and tipped all the cold water inside his shirt and down his belly. Now he had his pads on and the water could not get out of his trousers, so was coming out of his pockets and his fly front!! Jim recovered and hit the next ball for four, and we won the match.

Back at the pavilion, Bert Ward used to comment on your performance. He turned to me and said, 'well done Bob', and then he looked at the two who had got 'ducks' and said, 'you are better with one hand than some are with two!!' Jim then said, 'don't I get any word of thanks for 46 not out and winning the match?'

Bert replied, 'Yes, well done Jim, I will buy you a pint in the Devonshire.' Now Bert was well known for not spending anything if it could be at all avoided. Jim replied, 'I thought you would offer now as I can't stand at the bar in the Devonshire with water still coming out of my pockets and fly hole, everyone will think I've wet myself!!'

Now, when the cricket season came to an end, Fred and I continued to catch our usual amount of rabbits, as they were selling very well. One day, Fred had been in Ilkley and had seen a Mr Hampshire, who had a game dealer's in Brook Street. This was in late August, and he asked Fred if he could get him any partridge for the start of the season on 1st September.

Things were getting a bit more plentiful after the war, and he said some of his customers, the 'Toffs' in Ilkley, would love some partridge on the opening day and he would give us a good price for some.

Fred said he had seen some young partridge in the spring up by the pump field. So on 31st August 1948, we went to try and find them. I know they are not allowed to be shot before the opening day, but that mattered not the slightest to Fred if he could see a profit in the end.

Luck was with us as we saw a big covey of partridge fly in front of us and land in a field of fairly long grass, just below the old valve house below Chelker Reservoir.

We managed to get round behind the walls to where these birds had landed. When we got behind the last wall, the usual arrangement we had was that Fred being a left-handed shot and me a right, he shot any bird going right and I any going left, so that we didn't shoot at the same bird.

He looked over the wall and fired the first shot. I was up and at once ready to fire, but to my utter shock no birds flew away. Then one bird flew up about a yard and Fred shot this one, and reloaded his gun. In this moment, two others flew up about a yard and I shot them both.

This continued until no other birds flew up. We then got over the wall, with the dogs, and in the long grass the dogs found six brace of young partridge and one brace of old partridge. Fred explained to me that he must have shot both old birds with his first shot and the young birds had not then known what to do.

Fred took them to Hampshire's on the first morning, 1st September 1948, and received £8 a brace for the young birds and £6 a brace for the old ones. That was £54, and this was only the start of the season.

We continued to have great sport this back end and it will always go down in my memories as '1948, The Vintage Year'.

THE BEST YEAR YET, 1949

Now we start the year 1949, much the same as the last two years: working in the Crown and rabbit catching to provide my income.

Though I was not to know at the start of it, this year would change my life forever.

I was going to say 'for the worst', as I would have to start work soon, though on reflection, I have to say for the better for other reasons.

Tommy was still coming to the Crown and on some of his visits he would bring Fred an almost new suit. He was just Fred's build and they were always a perfect fit for him. Tommy used to get all these suits as a perk; as I've told you, he was a very well-known man in the wool trade. During this period, every male person would wear a dark suit, three-piece of course. These would be brown, dark tweed, black, pin stripe or similar, but no one had a light-coloured suit, nor would they be seen in one if they did have one!!

Fred was always well dressed: each evening behind the bar in a full suit with gold cufflinks, gold watch and chain; he was and looked the perfect landlord.

On this particular evening, he put on this fresh suit that Tommy had brought him; it was the most light-coloured suit anyone had seen at this time, yet he still looked the perfect landlord in it.

I will try to describe the colour: it was almost white, but in certain light looked blue, in another light it looked green. When he got behind the bar and all the usual customers came in, the remarks on this suit were fantastic. 'Where did you find that?', 'What a colour!', 'I would not be seen dead in it!', 'Which film are you in?' and so on.

At the end of the evening, when the pub was about to close, someone said, 'Now Fred, what colour do you call it?' Then, without a smile, or the sign of any hesitation, he said, 'DUCK EGG BLUE!' That name and suit lived with him for the rest of his life!!

Now, one day Fred had arranged with two other gunmen to go to a clay pigeon shoot at the New Inn in Appletreewick. These two local men were called Mr Berry, a retired cobbler from Addingham, and Joe Benson, a local clay pigeon shooter who was thought to be very good.

On the day of the shoot, they all met at the Crown, and had transport there and back arranged. However, for some reason Fred was unable to go, so he asked me to go in his place. Now, unknown to me, Joe Benson must have said something to Fred about me going, but I did not hear what he said.

All I heard was Fred say, 'You may be surprised.'

When the shoot started, we all had to shoot at 15 clay birds from a pigeon trap; I had been shooting at live rabbits running in and out of trees etc., so I found it fairly easy. The 15 birds were sent out one at a time, and I smashed all 15 first shot. At the end of this round, only four people had smashed 15. They were:

1   Myself
2   Mr Stitt (the head gamekeeper for the Duke of Devonshire)
3   Mr Berry
4   Joe Benson

The final round was one clay only in rotation, and if you missed you were out. I had first go and smashed mine, so did Mr Stitt, so did Mr Berry, but Joe Benson missed and was out.

Next round, I went first again and smashed mine, Mr Stitt then missed and Mr Berry smashed his. Now we should have shot another round but Mr Berry, who was old enough to be my grandfather, asked me if would I share the first and second prizes with him. I said yes as I thought he was a nice old man and would get a bit more money if I did share with him, as

I think he knew I would beat him anyway.

After the event, Mr Stitt came up to me and said, 'What is your name?' I said Robert Holmes from Addingham.

He replied 'Not another of those up-and-coming poachers!!'

When we got back to the Crown, Fred was waiting for us and he said to Joe Benson, 'Well, did you get a surprise?'

Joe Benson replied, 'You could have told me he was that good!!'

Now, in the Crown, when Fred was serving all the local lads, he had a nickname for each and every one. The names I can still remember are 'Sexton Blake', 'Frozen', 'Nail Crusher', 'Cartman' plus many others. This was alright until he gave you a tray of drinks to serve over the bar, and these would be all different, so he would then say, 'A pint of mild for Nail Crusher, a black and tan for Frozen and Sexton Blake only drinks halves so that is his, the half of bitter, and Cartman's is a pint of bitter.'

If you came back to the bar and had got it wrong, he would say aloud, 'What school did you go to?!!'

Yes, I soon got to be a good waiter.

Now, the one man who had the best nickname was a fine gentleman called Mr Croudson, who was also Fred's accountant. When he returned with Fred's book from audit, and said Fred would have a few pounds to pay, Fred would say to him, 'Mr Croudson, I thought you to be a good conservative; I now shall think of you as a worse thief than that communist Joe Stalin.' That's what he called him ever after!!

Now in early January, Aunt Eva had bought a small cottage, 13 Bolton Road, ready for Fred and her to retire into, but again Fred would not retire. I now know he was wrong not to do so. Because at this time, when I came in from a dance, I let myself into the Crown by the Bolton Road door. This one had a latch on and I had my own key for this door.

Once inside, I put the large bolts on and could have gone straight upstairs to bed, as the staircase was just to the left of this door. Though I always went into the kitchen first, and many times Aunt Eva was sat in the chair up to the little Yorkist range and coal fire. She was suffering badly from asthma and often had chest infections as well. The Crown had no central heating in those days and could be freezing, so I knew she spent many nights in that chair. The smoke and polluted atmosphere in the Crown was slowly killing her, so I did all I could to help her during the day.

I used to light all five fires in the Crown every day, and this was a job you had to get perfect at, as there was no firelighters then and all had to be lit with paper and wood.

On the cleaning side, I would get down many times and scrub all five floors on my knees for her, so she had only the dusting to do.

At closing time, when all the customers had gone, and if some seemed to be staying on longer than Fred thought was reasonable, he would say, 'Have you lot no homes to go to?!' and then they would all go home.

Bounce, Fred's dog, seemed to know when the last customer had gone: he could open the back door from outside and go and sit in front of the best fire that was still alight out of the five of them. I would let Chris in from the mortuary and the pair of them stayed for about an hour while we washed up and cleared all up. I then took Chris back to bed with a few biscuits and he was happy.

Aunt Eva used to try and send Bounce out into the stable, to sleep with the railway horse, but he would not go for her or for me. If Fred so much as smiled he would not move an inch, and Aunt Eva used to get mad with both Fred and Bounce.

Then, when Fred had allowed Bounce to get away with this for a few minutes, Fred would say to him, 'OUT', and he would go perfectly on one word of command.

I was in the Main Street one day in January, when a man I knew came up to me and asked me if I would like his job? His name was Horace Dingle, he was signalman at Addingham station. He had just got a good promotion to signalman at Gargrave but owing to the shortage of signalmen, he could not move until someone took his job.

He wanted to move as soon as possible as he wanted more money; he had a wife and family to support. He told me if I took the job for a month or two until he got to Gargrave, and then did not like it, I could still leave, as they could not recall him once he had moved on.

I knew the job was on the doorstep, so to speak, and that Fred and Eva would have to retire sometime. I thought I would try for it and went to see the then stationmaster, a man called Jack Newman, who later turned out to be a good friend to me.

After going to Leeds station for an interview, I got the job and started my training at Snaygill, south of Skipton and Niffany, north of Skipton, both mainline boxes.

I passed out as a qualified signalman after a few weeks and started work back at Addingham. The signal boxes that I had trained on had both been mainline boxes and were auto-locking boxes, but when I returned to Addingham it was an old LMS box with no safety features, so I had to teach myself about this old type.

The dances at the Crown had finished now, as the floor was moving about a lot and Fred decided in the end that it was really unsafe for so many people to be up there at the same time. Just off the end of the dance room was a small room, which was over part of the mortuary. A few pigeons had gone into this room through a pane of glass that was out of the window.

This small pigeon compartment was about six feet by four feet and was made inside a larger room especially as a pigeon loft. Who made it in the first place I do not know, as it was there in 1933, when Fred took over the Crown.

I hoped to try and rear a few pigeons in the spring, and maybe race a few that year, if possible.

However, on 14th February 1949, Valentine's day, a slightly more important thing happened that was to take up more of my time. On this night I had gone to the New Cinema dance hall in Ilkley after finishing at the Crown. We all had a grand evening at the dance and now was the time to go home to Addingham.

We had to get a taxi home, and as always this was Wilf Ettenfield's taxi. You paid one shilling each for your fare and no one got left behind. It did not matter if six or 16 of you got in the taxi, it was still one shilling each.

Some nights the numbers could be nearer 20.

Now I had been dancing most of the night with a girl called Jean Petty, who I had known since she was a small girl; in fact her father came in the Crown and had played cricket with my father.

The taxi was more than crowded and the first stop was New Road Top, where Jean was to get out. She happened to be sitting on my knee, with about six others, so just before we got to her stop I said to her, 'May I walk you home?', knowing she was the only one to get out at this stop. She said, 'Alright.'

Years later, she has often asked me, why did I chose that night? Now I will tell you the three reasons:

1   I could not breathe in that taxi, nothing to do with lovers' night!

2   I wanted to talk to Jean alone, as she was a fine woman of 25 and the most perfect blue-eyed blonde I had ever seen.

3   And now why I really chose that night: I had looked out of the taxi window and it was a fine dry moonlit, good-for-poaching night, and I knew when I walked from Church Street, where she lived back to the Crown, I would keep my demob suit dry!!

We got on well together, but I still had to work and also help at the Crown. Jean and I started going out together, and we used to go on our cycles to many places. One day I told her I'd take her somewhere she hadn't been before, which I did: up to Syreholme, to where the road finished, and then over the moorland track behind Simon Seat for some miles before the track came out at West End by the Old Village, which is now under Thruscross Reservoir.

It was a rough track at the best of times, and Jean had not been on this sort of ground on a cycle before, though I had been on Blubberhouses Moor years before. I said, 'you go first and slowly or you will fall off.' She kept going faster and I kept shouting for her to slow down. She kept saying, 'I'm perfectly alright.' Two seconds later, bang, and she crashed into the heather, bike as well. I laughed, not at her falling, but at the way she said she was alright. However, I picked her up and gladly, she was alright. We

then continued with the journey and completed it without any other accidents.

Today, we often pass the end of this old track or roadway and I remind her that not many women today will have ridden over there on a bike!

Working in the pub one evening, two men came in and asked Fred if he had any sporting guns for sale. He used to deal in one or two twelve-bore shot guns from time to time. On this day, he took the two fine-looking gentlemen into the snug and got them four guns to look at from the kitchen.

He came back to the bar and sent me into the snug with a drink each for these men. I served them, but at the same time I was watching them looking at the guns. On getting back to Fred in the bar, I told him those men are not genuine, they haven't a clue about what to look for in a gun. They should have been looking for the PROOF marks to say the guns were safe to use, and to see the barrels were not pitted, the stock was firm and many other features you look for. Although they were looking for the maker's name, always on the top rib of the barrels, they had not seen it. I said to Fred, 'I think they are plain clothes police officers!!'

Fred went back to the snug and I was right, two of the guns had been stolen in Ilkley.

Now Fred knew the young man he had bought them from, but also his mum, who lived up the Grove in Ilkley, and she was also related to the late Doctor Crabtree, who Fred had worked for many years before.

He went to see this lady the very next morning. She paid Fred back the price of the guns, plus another amount of cash if he would agree not to press charges against her son. He always had the luck to finish with everything to his advantage.

One night, many months after this episode, I called in the fish shop after being out and got some fish and chips, and seeing this was only across the road from the Crown, I took them with me to eat in the kitchen. Fred and Aunt Eva had gone to bed, and I had the fish and chips on the table straight from the paper.

I could not believe what I saw on this paper, as it was a newspaper from up Durham way. The report stated that this man had gone into a hotel and ordered dinner for about 30 soldiers and had run off without paying the bill. It was the same man who had stolen those guns and sold them to Fred. He had been sent to prison for six months.

I left the paper on the table, and a note for Fred to read it next morning: the comment from him was that it was bound to happen!!

About March of this year, I had got together a few pigeons in the old room at the Crown, including three old ones, all hens, that I had rung and reared the year before.

Some afternoons after I'd finished my early shift at the station, I would go round to an old pigeon fancier called Harry Whitaker, who was also a first-class joiner and the local undertaker. I liked joinery work and when he was busy and when he had a few funerals, at nearly the same time, he was glad of the help. All oak then, nothing on the cheap to bury anyone in.

I didn't get or expect any pay, I was happy to learn from him. However, he said one day that he was going to Silsden that evening and would make me a member of Silsden Pigeon Club and would pay my subscriptions.

The next week he told me I would require a pigeon clock, so that I could race the following month, and that he knew a Mr Binns, of Middleton at Cowling, who had a few clocks for sale.

So I went over to Cowling, on my bike, and bought a clock, a Toulet 12 Bird 135492; I can still remember the number. And Mr Binns showed me how to use it and how it was set for racing.

On the Tuesday, Harry said are you sending any pigeons on Friday, because if you are you can go to Silsden with me. I sent three hens all feeding large youngsters: the worst condition possible, I was later told.

On the Saturday, the day of the race, Harry told me not to go round to his loft, which was next to his joiner's shop, until I had clocked a pigeon or I could miss one.

It was raining very heavily when the pigeons should have arrived back, but just as I thought I would give up, a dark white flight hen came in through the window and I put the rubber ring it was wearing in the clock. I then went round to Harry's to see how many he had before me as he had sent well over a dozen. On seeing me come out of the joiner's shop and into the pigeon pen, he said, 'I told you not to come round here until you'd clocked in.' I said, 'But I have, at 3.20 pm.' He had none home, and then said, 'well go back, you may get another.' I said, 'That is too late; it came when I was walking down the steps!!'

I went to Silsden that evening to find I had won first from Nottingham: the first race I had ever entered. This was to start me racing for the next ten years, and with great success.

We had now got to late April or early May and I was about to start the cricket season with Bolton Abbey, when on this particular day Aunt Eva said to me that she was going to sell 13 Bolton Road, as she said yet again that Fred would not retire.

So I thought seriously about this, because if anything happened to Fred and Eva in the future, I would be back in my old position with no home to go to. I asked her to sell it to me, which she did for £359.

Now I had been going out with Jean on a regular basis since February, but this was not yet common knowledge in the village. She used to pass the Crown every day on her way to work at Townhead Mill as a weaver, even at lunchtimes she would walk, cycle or almost run up and down the street in the short time allowed for lunch.

So the day after Eva said I could have the house, I stopped Jean on her way back to work at lunchtime, and told her I had thought about buying a house and would she call on her way home from work, if she would like to look at it.

We went to look at the house together and I said to her if she was prepared to live in this house we could get engaged the following weekend, and then get married as soon as we had got it ready to live in. Of course, you all know her answer was YES!

Now I have thought many times about the previous two years to this, just think about it. In the previous two and a quarter years I had made almost enough money with rabbiting and poaching to buy a house!

I wonder how many unemployed people today could do that in just over two years!

Together we started to get this house ready to live in, and it also got around the village that these two people were being seen around the village together and were getting married shortly.

Of course, everyone speculated on the outcome of these two people being together and many said it would be the biggest mismatch of the century.

You see, Jean's family were Church of England. Her father was the vicar's warden, Jean herself was a Sunday school teacher and all the family went to church regularly on Sundays.

I was known at the time as an idle young man, who had been out of work for over two years and did not want any. The totally wrong type for that nice young lady!

You could not, of course, tell everyone that you had earned more money on a Monday morning before breakfast than they would do all week!

Poachers don't want the taxman to know that!

Though Jean was to get to know all one night when she called at the fish shop across from the Crown to take fish and chips home to her family. The shop was full, and when Jean got to the counter to be served by Harry Gill, the owner, he said to her, 'Is it right you are going to marry Bob Holmes?' She said, 'Yes.' To which he answered, 'Well if you are marrying him, I suppose

A KNOWN NOWT'S BETTER THAN AN UNKNOWN NOWT.'

Several weeks later, she went in the fish shop, on her own again, and yet again it was full of his customers. When Harry Gill said to Jean, 'So you are going to marry Bob are you, after all?', Jean replied, 'YES, I am.'

Harry: 'Well he is a bit of a rough diamond but if he says he will marry you he will, and not leave you, and you will always have a bit of money in your purse, but *you* will HAVE TO EARN IT.'

So, over the following weekend, we went to Skipton and bought an engagement ring from the jeweller's in the high street. Looking at the trays of rings in the shop I had seen the one that to my unqualified eyes appeared to be far and away the best in the price range we had together arranged to pay. Then Jean said, 'I like that one.' It was the same ring I had already selected. So this was the ring we chose.

On Jean wearing this ring during the next few weeks, many of her friends would say what a good ring she had got and many would have been wondering how I had been able to afford to get one of this quality. Yet many years later there is an answer to many things about this ring and that I will tell later.

Jean arranged for us to go to her church and see about the wedding arrangements. We talked awhile as the vicar knew both of our families, Jean's more than mine.

Though, really, Jean was the 'Off cum'd en', having only lived in Add- ingham from being six months old, but my family history has been traced back in Addingham to the year 1410!

However, we got round to talking about the wedding, when the vicar said, 'What time do you want to get married?' My reply really caught him out when I said, 'What time do you get up?' He replied '8.30 am.' My an- swer: 'We will therefore get married at 9.00 am!'

'Engaged.'

So our wedding day arrived and we got married in St Peter's Church, Addingham, on 9th August 1949, at 9.00am. Ernest, Jean's brother, was my best man. Ernest's girlfriend, Dorothy, was Jean's bridesmaid along with Freda, Jean's younger brother's wife. Now the time of the wedding did not suit all members of both families, but the Crown had to be open at 11.30 am the same day, as the licence hours for hotels were very strict in those days.

P

Mr. & Mrs. Petty
request the company of

....

at the marriage of their daughter

Jean, with Mr. Robert Holmes,

at St. Peter's Church, Addingham,
on Tuesday, August 9th, 1949, at 9-0 a.m.,
and afterwards at The Blue Bird Café.

Church Street,
Addingham.   R.S.V.P.

We had the reception at the Blue Bird Café in Ilkley, before returning to the Crown. This was on a Tuesday. Jean and I could not afford much of a honeymoon after furnishing our little cottage, so my mum said we could stay a night or two at Swinton, which we did, before returning to our home at 13 Bolton Road.

We both started work the following Monday and by Christmas of that year we had finished furnishing our home, so this had to be THE BEST YEAR YET, 1949.

'Cutting the cake.'

THE LAST STATIONMASTER

Jean and I then settled down in this small cottage and both of us continued to work, though Jean was earning more money that I was because weavers were in demand and textiles were selling well. Chris moved into the cottage with us but would not stay at night, about 9 o'clock he would go to the door and shake himself to let you know he required his biscuits and you had to take him back to his bed in the mortuary.

This cottage was to be the very best house we ever lived in for saving money, it was only 1s/9d a week in rates, including water!

Chris used to like to sit on the step outside our cottage, but it was not long before we found out the reason he was keen to do this.

When ladies came to the Co-op, which was directly across the road from us, he would watch them leave their prams outside as they could not get them up the three large steps into the shop.

They could see the baby outside through the large window as they were being served, and used to give the child a biscuit to stop it from crying.

When the child looked into the shop to see where its mother had gone, the child would let its hand containing the biscuit fall over the side of the pram. Chris would wait for this moment and then very slowly and gently take the biscuit from the child's fingers without it knowing.

When the child looked round at its hand for the biscuit, it was missing and it would scream for its mum. The mum used to then turn the pram inside out looking for the biscuit, but to no avail.

When at home, Jean spent her time replacing the biscuits!

Fred and Eva were still in the Crown and we both used to go and help them in the evening.

I again started the cricket season with Bolton Abbey, when us young men used to meet in the back bar of the Devonshire before going to the match. We could only have a half a shandy each as the older players used to make sure we got served no more. We used to pick up two older men called Harry Wood and Fred Metcalfe who were both very interested in the team. We used to ride to the field on bikes and these two got a ride in one of the cars.

The barmaid in the bar used to change every few weeks as the staff did not seem to stay very long. On this day, a new one had taken over and we had never seen a local girl like this. She was a very well-made girl in all departments, with bright shoulder-length ginger hair and an even brighter pink blouse open almost to her waist.

When we went out of the bar to go to the match, Fred and Harry used to come out for their lifts.

Though on this occasion, only Fred came out, and someone said, 'Is Harry not coming?' Fred said at once, 'No he is not, he has been sat at that bar all dinnertime, GLOWERING AT THAT LASS LIKE A BLOODY OLD TOM CAT!!'

On another occasion we had a meeting of the club one evening in the bar, it must have been special because we had them in the pavilion at normal times.

During this meeting, one or two of the team had gone over the road into the farmyard where old Tom Roe used to leave his horse and cart after finishing his rounds, and have a few pints. Someone bought him a few pints more, while the others took his horse out of the shafts, put the shafts through the farm gate and harnessed her up on the other side. The gate was now between the horse and cart and it would not move.

When old Tom came out and saw the situation, the lads were behind the wall. When Tom had had a few pints he used to stutter when excited and he then blamed Old Polly the horse, saying: 'Now P-P-P-POLLY you are in a P-P-P-PROPER P-P-P-PREDICAMENT T-T-T-TONIGHT!!'

The lads helped him sort it out and I take it he then sobered up on his way home to Addingham.

It was now well into 1950 and I had worked over a year as a signal-man; I liked the job as I worked early shifts most of the time so had plenty of time to do other things.

I then rented a plot of land from the Railway Land Agents and put up a proper pigeon loft which was right next to the station. I was also helping Harry in the joiner's shop and he kept giving me small young pigeons a week or so old, to rear under some of my own.

These always turned out to be dark check, with an unusual touch of bronze.

I raced these pigeons in Silsden and District Flying Club, North West Yorkshire Federation, Bradford Championship Club. I had great success over the next nine years or so with these birds, winning in all the above clubs.

I once asked Harry what strain these birds were, and he said 'MONS GURNAY', but when I asked how he got them he just walked away. It was some years before Harry died, and then after that, talking to a local man, I found out all the history of these pigeons; I will come back to that later. The best pigeon I ever raced was one I bred in 1952: it was a big check-ered cock, number 1027. In 1955, as a three year old, I sent it in every race, that was nine inland races and three Channel races from France. The prizes were first, second, third, fourth and pool pigeon. This pigeon won me money in ten races out of 12. Some pigeon, so much so that many fanciers would not pool against this bird!

In early 1952, Jack Newman, the stationmaster, got a promotion to take over the post of stationmaster at Newlay and Horsforth. We had no relief stationmaster for a few months, so I did the accounts each month end and had to balance these to $^{1}/2$d. At this time, we received quite a substantial amount of cash for passengers' tickets and from many larger accounts from the mills that would send cloth by rail. This we sent on the train each day, in a leather bag sealed with the old red sealing wax, to Ilkley where it had to be taken intact to the Midland Bank. We got the empty bag each afternoon. One Monday, I sent the bag as usual when during the day the bank manager telephoned to say I had put four shillings short in the bag. He said it was two two-shilling pieces that were short.

Both the porter and myself knew we were correct because we had a problem finding the correct change.

However, after I had a strong argument with the manager, he got mad and said, 'Send me the money tomorrow, Tuesday, BANKS DON'T MAKE MISTAKES,' and put the phone down.

I sent the money on the Tuesday, but I was still not happy. On the Friday each week, when the bag was returned from the bank, it contained the wages for all the staff. That was the platelayers, porters and myself.

On the same Friday as I had the disagreement with the bank manager, after we paid out the wages, the porter and myself found we had two one- pound notes too many.

Not long after we found this out the same manager came on the phone saying he had put this amount wrong in the bag.

So I told him, 'Just one moment, it was only on Monday you told me in no uncertain terms that BANKS DON'T MAKE MISTAKES', and I hung up the phone on him! The porter and myself had a pound each extra that week.

Now the position of stationmaster was again put on the notice board of the vacancies we used to receive, so I thought that as I was doing most of the job, I would apply for it. It was not a job I should have gone for as it was a clerical job and not the manual type I was doing. I should have gone for higher jobs as a signalman.

However, I did not really care if I got an interview or not because I was happy in both my job and at home.

Within a day or two, though, I had word back from the head office in

Leeds to go for an interview. So I went for this interview with not a care in the world. On-going before this interview board of these men, I could soon tell they did not know very much about the running of a small village station. They kept asking me questions about how to do the station accounts.

After a while, I said to them, 'Excuse me gentlemen, but I have been doing the accounts for the last three months and have had no complaints, but there is much more to a local stationmaster's job than accounts, things like unloading bulls and farm animals that come by rail, being among the local tradespeople, and we are getting more business for the railway in parcels than most stations do in passengers.'

I noticed the shocked look on their faces at this outburst, when one of them said let him have the job. So the job was mine and, at the age of 27, I was one of the youngest stationmasters on British Rail.

Though stationmaster, I continued to do the signal box work for about one hour a day, each afternoon about 2.00 pm when the goods train arrived from Guiseley on its way back to Skipton. This then left us the wagons of coal ordered by the coal merchants and cattle for farmers, timber or other goods.

One day, this train came to us and had only one wagon of coal to drop for us. Now the signalman is only responsible for the main lines and when in the sidings this goes under the guard's orders. I had noticed the platelayers doing some work that week on the points in the yard, and I thought they looked different from the week before but I was not too sure. So I opened the signal box window as I was going to warn the guard, when he was most rude and told me he was in charge of the yard and to close the window, which I did.

He then knocked off this wagon of coal and it should have gone up to the other coal wagons in the yard, but it did not. It went up the goods shed track and straight through the wooden door, through the goods shed and the door at the other end of the shed, both in a thousand pieces, and into the buffers at the top so hard that over two tonnes of coal bounced out onto the ground!

He went back to Skipton to report the accident, very red indeed!

One day, while waiting on the platform with the porter for a train to arrive from Ilkley, going to Bolton Abbey, we helped everyone to board the train and collected tickets from those getting off. We got a shock from one of the passengers on board.

On the platform stood a lady, shouting, 'Will you please help me'. I looked and saw it was a lady called Miss Wall, a farmer in Addingham, holding a rope attached to something still in the carriage.

Everyone went to help, including the guard. Inside the carriage was the largest TUP I have ever seen, it was the size of a donkey. After some pushing and pulling we finally got it onto the platform, and the train then departed a few minutes late. The guard must have said something to Miss Wall as I saw her show him a piece of paper still in her hand.

On leaving the platform to walk the TUP home, she showed me the same paper, no wonder the guard looked shocked, so did I when I saw it was a ticket for the TUP.

FROM THE MIDLANDS TO ADDINGHAM FIRST CLASS FOR THE TUP! AS A PASSENGER!

One day, while working at the station, a lady asked me if she could put some goats on the land between the railway platform and Southfield Road. This land belonged to the railway company but was growing long grass and looked a bit untidy. I therefore agreed to her request and the goats could not get onto Southfield Road as it had a strong wooden fence all the way down the road side.

One of the goats then had two young kids, and being so near the village, everyone used to come and feed them. One day, one of the young kids got through the wire fence onto the platform. It had then walked off the platform end onto the railway line. At the very moment I saw it, the goods train from Ilkley to Bolton Abbey was coming full steam through the station and I had no chance to do anything as the engine, six wagons and the guard's van went straight over the young kid.

Just then Austin, the porter, came round the corner and I told him what had happened, and as the kid was now looking dead between the sleepers, he had better get the spade as we would have it to bury before the lady owner, who was a very sentimental old dear, arranged a goat's funeral on the platform.

He went to dig a hole on the railway banking and I went for a sack to put the kid in, which was about the size of a small dog.

On-going to pick the kid up and put it into the sack, I noticed its eye lids were still open though its eyes showed only complete white with no pupils showing at all.

Just then, from under its top eyelids, its pupils started to appear in a downward direction. When it could see it then moved its ears, then shook itself and stood up.

I carried it back to its mother and the lady never knew anything about it. So I could be one of the few people who have tried to bury a live GOAT! Yes, so very NEAR!!

We had moved now from our little cottage to the large semi-detached station house, which was to be our home for the next ten years.

Just before moving, a man, who had heard about our move, came to see us at the cottage and asked how much we wanted for it, before we had even decided to sell. He went home after we told him the amount we would be asking and returned a few minutes later, with the cash in his hand.

Jean had left weaving now, I had told her to get a less dirty job, so she applied and got a job at Hardingham's in Brook Street in Ilkley and also worked in their Ben Rhydding Shop. This was the best local confectioners around at the time, and she was very happy behind a counter and meeting people.

I now had to give up any cricket as I was on duty on certain Saturdays, and in any case, I wanted to go into pigeon racing and showing in a more serious way.

During this period, Joe Hargrave started to help me race pigeons. He was later to keep show pigeons with great success. He was a first-class painter and decorator, having served his time at the trade with my Uncle Arthur, who was my father and Uncle Fred's younger brother.

Now Arthur, who had played rugby for Yorkshire in the front row and during the first war had won high awards for bravery in France and Belgium, was a hard task master, though Joe suffered his apprenticeship with him, it is more than I could have done. Joe told me this story about him.

One Monday during the war, just Arthur and Joe were left as all of his other men had gone to the war. Mr and Mrs Lumley, who were both on the council, came to ask them to come and decorate the staircase in their large farmhouse before Friday, as they were holding a council meeting at their home that night. That should have been easy, except they had no wallpaper or paint left owing to shortages in the war.

The pair of them somehow mixed some concoction and went to complete the work. All the time this was in progress, Mrs Lumley stood at the bottom of the stairs having her say and directing operations. Arthur then said, 'That's it, we've finished.' Mrs Lumley replied, 'YES, it will DO until the next time.'

Arthur: 'Mrs Lumley, their won't be a bloody next time!', and that was a customer! Joe should have had a gold medal for working with him!

I continued racing pigeons with the help of Joe and, later, Bert Wilkinson, an old pigeon man, came to help me as Harry the joiner had now died and up to that point Bert had been Harry's right-hand man with the pigeons.

One race I do recall was the first young bird race of the season, about 1954 or so, a big bunch of young birds came together up the village, many for Silsden and Skipton and for the village. Many birds started to pull out of this bunch and four flew straight into my loft. Joe and I took the rubber rings from the birds and Jean and Joan, our wives, put the rings into the thimbles and Bert clocked them in.

We won the first four positions in the club and the first four positions in the federation. This was a very large federation then, from Skipton to the far side of Bradford.

Though the reason this was so special was we had all four rings in the clock in just seven seconds!

Now about this time, I got talking to an old man called Harry Ellis, who I thought worked in Ilkley as a gardener, about his pigeons, when I found he had been a great friend of Harry Whitaker, the joiner, who I think had gone to school with him.

He then told me how Harry had obtained the 'GURNAY' pigeons. At the time, only two men were racing these birds with great success,

O.I. Wood of Ilkley and Fred Shaw of Manchester. It is recorded in pigeon books about these two men's outstanding performances, but what was not known at the time was that these two men were racing the unknown widowhood racing system. Now O.I. Wood was a very wealthy man and lived in Middleton at Ilkley, where he had servants, gardeners and pigeon loft men. Now on the widowhood system, pigeons do not race to eggs or young birds, but only to the hen that each cock is paired to. So that if any eggs are laid these are surplus and are thrown out.

Harry Ellis was picking up all the surplus eggs from the compost heap and Harry the joiner reared every young bird that hatched from them. No wonder these pigeons were the best racing at that time. One of the best single results was to come in the last young bird race from Folkestone in 1956. A young hen, number 302, won first club and first federation and second in all Yorkshire on that day. I won a trophy, over £50 in cash and a lovely canteen of cutlery in this one race. As a matter of interest to pigeon fanciers, 302 was the daughter of 1027.

Getting to know if you had won in those days was not so quick, no computers, etc. then. Though on coming through Bradford on my motorbike on the Sunday after the race, Jean saw a pigeon fancier walking down the street. I shouted, 'Who won the Federation from Folkestone?' Although he did not see me he shouted 'A b------ called Holmes from Addingham!'

That was all I wanted to hear. Later, I said to Jean, who had seen the man even from riding on the pillion, 'How did you know he was a pigeon man in Bradford?' She replied 'He had a pigeon feather stuck to the Brylcream on his wavy hair just like you often have.'

By the way, the motorbike I bought new in about 1955 was a BSA 250 in a 350 frame. It had a sidecar frame, which we put a box on to carry the pigeons, but we used to take this off when on holiday and Jean and I rode miles together SOLO.

Now the platelayers working on the railway at this time consisted of Jack Longfellow from Ilkley, the ganger, and three men from Addingham, Jim Roe, Norman Wall and Cecil Ellen (the same lad who drove me across the Suez Canal a few years before).

Jack used to walk the track from Ilkley each morning to knock in the wood blocks into the chairs that the rails were held by. These had to be done every day as some came out in dry weather.

Now Cecil was never at work when Jack arrived from Ilkley. He would be late every single day but he had a different excuse every time. He had a young family already and his wife always seemed to be expecting again. So their excuses were perfect: 'She has morning sickness' and he had to wash and cook for the children and get them ready for school.

Jack had enough of his tales and told him if he was late tomorrow, he would sack him.

Now all the men were working about half a mile up the line towards Bolton Abbey, and I was passing them going to change a signal lamp, when who should come walking up the line but Cecil: this was ten to nine in the morning and not starting time of ten past seven. Jack's question to him: 'What's your excuse for today, Cecil?' 'No excuse Jack, I left home at seven o'clock and Walker's bull was on the line and I have waited an hour and a half to get past it!'

Some days later, when Jack was walking the line to Bolton Abbey and back, he had seen one of Lumley's hens laying away on the line side. He waited until it had laid 13 eggs, then collected them and brought them to the station in his cap.

His men, the platelayers, were working between the platforms in the station, which could be a dangerous place. A train was now approaching and Jack shouted, 'Get out of there!' Jim and Norman climbed out onto the platform but Cecil, who was a lot younger, put his hands on the edge of the platform and sprung up backwards, also onto the platform, though what he did not see behind him was Jack's cap with the 13 eggs in it. He landed with his behind directly into Jack's cap!

We all laughed but Jack was not amused and said, 'Cecil, you have ruined my cap.' Cecil replied, 'No I haven't, the whites of the egg will make it stick better to your bald head!!'

The station was still very busy at this time, early 1958, with the 'Olicana Windscreens' being sent all over from the High Mill, plants from the market gardeners and still cloth from the mills.

This year, 1958, saw the pigeon men form Addingham Homing Society, which also brought parcels and traffic to the station.

At the beginning of this year, I rode the motorbike one Saturday night, with Jean on the pillion, down to Swinton, South Yorkshire, to see MUM as she was poorly.

I had to ride it home that night as I was at work on the Sunday with special-trip trains.

However, it started to snow on the way home and we had to come over Heath Common (no motorways then!), and when we got home I was hours thawing out. I threw the bike down and said, 'That's it, I will not ride it again.' I sold it shortly afterwards and bought a new A35 van.

Now, at the end of 1958, I sold all my racing pigeons (except a few I gave to my friend Joe) at a large sale in Birmingham.

Both Joe and myself had agreed we would from now on go into showing pigeons in a big way.

This we could do in both summer and winter and, as good money could be won in both, we really fancied our chances.

Now 1958 was at a close, and the next four years brought more changes than I ever expected. One was I would be THE LAST STATIONMASTER IN ADDINGHAM!

A GREAT CHANGE FOR US ALL

The next four years started in 1958 and before this period was out in 1962, Jean and I were not to know that this was to be a time of

'A great change for us all!'

First Joe Petty, Jean's father, gave me a few practical tips and help with my early driving. He had driven buses all through the wartime blackout, so was the best teacher I could have found.

I had driven our motorbike for years, so knew the road markings, etc., and had also driven an ambulance a few times in the war (no licence, of course!).

So when I wished to go out before taking my driving test, Uncle Fred would sit with me as he had a licence from before the First World War, but had not driven for going on 30 years. In fact, he taught the local doctor to drive, in the third car in Addingham in fact.

That gave you no confidence at all, as on that occasion he would tell you they came down Murk Hill at Bolton Abbey at great speed, BACK-WARDS!!

On our very first journey together we were going to Otley, I cannot now remember the reason, but going up Church Street in Ilkley I stopped at the pedestrian crossing for a lady. The lady was at the offside of the road and walked across the crossing, then in front of the van and to Fred's side of the road. Before I knew what he was doing he had the side window down at his side and called the dear lady all the stupid fools he could think of for crossing the road in front of a car. The lady was in order, but was so shocked at his outburst she ran off into one of the shops.

On reaching the traffic lights at Brook Street, I stopped again as the lights were on red. Fred said, 'What's the matter now?' I said the lights are at red. He replied, 'Well nothing's coming, get going!'

We got through Burley without any other event, but on entering by the mill in Otley, at the last moment, a black cat ran straight under the van, this was not lucky. I heard a bump and knew I'd killed it and looking through the mirror I saw this to be so. I hesitated as if to stop, when he shouted, 'Keep going, that's some more vermin out of the way!'

I passed my test first time in Skipton, and felt safer already without Fred being with me.

Jean had now gone to work at the Co-op in Bolton Road, Addingham, and being nearer to home we could go out together much more often.

In the early months of 1959 we got a shock when Jean was going to have a baby. When the baby was due to be born we would have been married almost ten years. Seeing that this was almost certain to be our only chance to have a family, as Jean would be 37 by the time the baby was born, we arranged for her to go as a private patient under Mr Graham at Keighley Victoria Hospital. Jean was still working at the Co-op when her accident there in early May almost ruined all our hopes. There was a large trapdoor in the back room at the Co-op, also the same trapdoor on all three floors, as this had been used regularly in years gone by to lift grain and flour, etc. from floor to floor, as a lot of packing used to be done in the shop premises in those days.

On this particular day, someone opened the door to the cellar and did not inform the shop staff. As Jean went into the back to get something for a customer, she stepped back and went backwards into the cellar, an eight-foot drop.

Someone came rushing up to me at the station and after seeing she was not badly hurt, but bleeding from a head wound, I got the van and took her to Victoria Hospital rather quickly.

Her head wound required about four stitches, and then I brought her home. She spent the next few days in bed and very luckily no harm came to the baby.

About this time, the coalman, who I knew well, asked me if I would take his wife round Skipton in their car as he did not have time to teach her to drive. The lady's name was Edith Blagborough, she was older than Jean and me, and had a boy and girl at school.

I arranged to start taking her round Skipton the following Monday. By the way, the car was her husband's, a large Humber Hawk, the worst possible to learn to drive in. After we had been round Skipton, we pulled up on about the third time round for me to point out another mess she was making on one corner. She said to me, 'I will get that right on Friday, when I take my TEST!!' I would not have put her in for a test in a month of FRIDAYS!!

Anyway, the Friday arrived and away she went with the test examiner; I was only hoping she got him back in one piece. They finally arrived and then walked together into the test centre. She came out ten minutes later, running towards me and waving a paper, shouting, 'I'VE PASSED'. I was speechless, I just couldn't believe it.

Before she left me at home to go and give her husband the good news, I told her now you are on your own do not take this large car where you cannot get it out of, as the first few times on your own you could have problems.

Now, on the Monday afternoon following the Friday when she passed, the phone went in the station office. It was Edith asking me if I would go and ask her husband who was working in the station coal yard, if he would go to Skipton with the coal wagon and pull the car off some railings she had managed to get the car fast on. Eddie, her husband, did so, but left part of the car still fast to the railings! So much for TEST EXAMINERS! Shirley was born shortly after this in Victoria Hospital, Keighley. I took Jean into the hospital and while there Mr Graham told me he was more concerned for the baby than for Jean. So it was no surprise to me when he informed me that Jean had had to have Caesarean section, that the baby GIRL was fine and Jean was also alright but would take time to get thoroughly back to normal. He said I could visit the hospital and see them both.

I set off for the hospital at once, but not before I had sent the usual bouquet of flowers (Interflora, of course). I was in no way going into any hospital with a bunch of flowers. I still refuse to do that, so don't go into hospital and expect any from me!

Shirley helps Santa.

When entering the hospital, a sister came to me and said, 'You can see the baby girl now, before you go and see your wife.' I was surprised to see how lovely she looked, with beautiful pink and white skin, not at all wrinkled, as I had been lead to believe.

While writing this it has come to me that Shirley will very soon be 40, so the wrinkles will be appearing shortly, DEAR!

In about ten days, I brought Jean and the baby girl home and though everyone kept asking 'what are you going to call her', we had already decided. Everybody had kept saying boys' names before she was born, but I had every confidence she would be a girl, and the name had been chosen by us long before she was born. We thought that

Shirley Ann Jacqueline Holmes would make a fine signature, a lot better than ours, Bob and Jean.

When Jean fully recovered and been at home a few months, the manager at the Co-op asked her if she could go back to work part time over Christmas. Now my mum was a widow, as her second husband, my stepfather, had just died, so she said she would love to come and stay and help with the baby if Jean wanted to go back to the Co-op. Jean then started back at the Co-op and Fred and Eva had at last retired to a small cottage in the Malt Kiln Yard, which was in fact the back-to-back cottage to the one at 13 Bolton Road, where we had first started married life.

All this property has since been pulled down and is now a car park.

Now about the early part of 1960, the railways were being run down ready for the man called Dr Beeching, who was shortly to ruin the railways of England for the next 40 years. If ever a man cost this country millions he was the one, for all the goods and traffic he put onto our roads in the NEXT 40 years. If the cost of repairing all these roads and bridges was added together it would have been cheaper to pay him in gold and put him on the first ship back to America.

So knowing the small stations would close sometime in the near future, we were thinking again about our future when the unexpected happened again.

On this particular day in early 1960, I saw in the Ilkley Gazette an advert for a small house and shop at 143 Main Street in Addingham. This shop was now closed and had been for some time, but had nevertheless been a good little shop when I was a boy.

So knowing that Jean had always wanted a shop of her own, I went to Ilkley and into the estate agents' who were selling it. That was what is now Dacre Son and Hartley's, but it was Doug Hartley who was in charge then; he had auctioned any property for sale at the Crown years before. I then asked about this property and Doug Hartley came out to see me.

He said someone was coming to view late that afternoon, so I asked if it was possible for me to have the key if I were to return it before 2 o'clock. He was not too sure about this, so I told him that I knew the lad who had been living rough in this house and was aware I wouldn't be looking at a palace. With this, he let me have the key. I called in the Co-op to see Jean on my way home and told her I had got the key to the shop and that she could see it in her lunch hour, but I wanted to know if she would like to go into business or not as I had to return the key by 2.00 pm!!

So we looked together in the lunch hour and it was a tip alright, but she was prepared to have a go, so I was also prepared to give her my full support.

I went back to Ilkley with the key and said I would buy the house and shop at the price stated.

So as I was signing my cheque to pay for it, a man I knew came into the estate agents', from Addingham, who also wanted to buy the same property, but he was too late, it was sold!

We then started to get the shop and house ready during the next few months. The shop we sorted first, as this was the place we wanted to open first. Ken, Jean's youngest brother, removed the fireplace for us and did all the plumbing work required, he is a first-class plumber by trade who had then turned to teaching. We had local joiners in to do the shop fitting and Joe (the same lad who helped with the pigeons, and many more tales about Joe you will hear yet) and myself did all the painting.

Jean opened the shop in September 1960, though we continued to live in the station house and I carried on as stationmaster for the time being. Just as we were going to start getting the house at 143 Main Street ready to live in, the other house (145 Main Street) of the semi-detached block of property came up for sale.

Again I rushed down to Dacre Son and Hartley. When Mr Hartley came into the reception area I told him I had come about the house, 145 Main Street, and told him I was good enough to buy 143 Main Street in the state it was in, that it was only right he should give me first chance of the other half of this property.

He agreed and said I could have until the following evening to let him know if I wanted to buy it.

I was going to buy it anyway, but mum had said she would like to return to Addingham sometime, so I rang her that evening and she said to buy it for her. We then had to start in this house, getting it ready for her to move into and leave 143 for the time being.

Mum moved back to Addingham in early 1961.

Jean was now starting to build up a nice amount of business in the shop, and we could see some future in it together. So we then made another special effort and got 143 Main Street ready for us to live in.

So in January 1962, I resigned as stationmaster at Addingham, to go and help Jean in the shop. I had been at the station almost thirteen years to the day, three as signalman and the rest as stationmaster.

Before leaving the station house I arranged for my porter, Austin Burdock, to live in it. He and his family later bought it.

Austin remained at the station as the porter until it closed in 1965, but no stationmaster was ever appointed after I resigned.

So this period was to be 'A Great Change for us All'.

SHOWING FOR PROFIT

From 1959, and for the next three years, Joe Hargrave and myself had decided we would have a go at 'Showing for Profit'.

We started with the winter shows, when we used all the Gurnays we had then retained, and continued in the summer round the northern agricultural shows with the proper show pigeons.

Of course, we changed these types of birds round on several occasions when we thought the judge would not be skilled enough to tell the difference; many were not.

One of the first shows we had great success at was the Oxenhope Open Show, held at the Lamb Inn in Oxenhope. Now I was friendly with John Ambler, who knew I had won best in show the previous year: when I arrived, he said, 'You haven't brought those Gurnays again have you?' I replied, 'Only one,' which was true.

I in fact had a Gurnay cock that we called the 'Brasso Cock' because unlike the normal Gurnays which were all dark with slight bronze marking on the feather ends, this one was the only one I had ever bred that had the colours the other way round. Being mainly bronze when the sun shone on this cock, it did look as though you had cleaned it with Brasso. After entering my birds, I saw I had a pen that was at the top of the stairs in front of the staircase window, so I put this 'Brasso Cock' in this pen and hoped the sun would shine.

Now John asked me if I would sell some raffle tickets for him downstairs in the pub. I agreed to do so but asked what the prizes were, to which he replied, 'the usual bottles but the first is that mystery prize in the brown box.' I was just going to move this box for some reason, when John said, 'don't move it as it's alive.'

I then knew what was in the box, as I had heard a noise like a pup.

'What breed is it, John?' I asked, and he replied, 'a Jack Russell, but don't tell anyone.'

Downstairs, I sold a lot of tickets, but on going into one of the front rooms to sell a few more, who should be sitting there but one of my club members from Silsden. He asked me, 'What are the prizes, Bob?' I told him the usual bottle and a mystery prize. 'What's that Bob?' was a typical Silsden reply. So as not to tell anyone I just pointed my finger at the dog he had with him.

He then turned to the lady sitting next to him, who also had a dog, 'You don't want another dog do you?' Her reply, 'NO.'

'Then if I win bring me a bottle', was his reply. I then knew that this lady he was with was not his wife! How could he have gone for a walk with one dog and returned with two?

When John drew the raffle the man from Silsden did win first prize so I took him the bottle he said he wanted.

John then drew the next ticket, which was mine, so I was just thinking what to do with this pup in this box when another man from another room came to see what was in the box. On seeing this pup, he said, 'That's just what I want, can I buy it?' I said, 'I may sell it.' When at once he said, 'I will give you £25 for it.' So I sold it to him, very quickly.

It was not long before the show was over when someone shouted, 'You can all come up stairs.'

Of course, with John always being the first upstairs to see the results, he rushed up the first three or four steps, looked up and then stopped in his tracks when he saw at the top of the stairs the 'Brasso Cock' with the pen covered in prize cards and best in show yet again. He turned and saw me at the bottom of the stairs and just said, 'You and those blasted Gurnays!' Not a bad start to the show season; best in show plus a dog sold for £25!

The next big show we decided to go to was the West Riding Federation Open Show held at Hebden Bridge. This was in a pub or club called The

Neptune which had a canal just a few yards from the back door and it would have been easy to finish in the canal if you had too much to drink. This place may have been pulled down, as I cannot now find it.

The show had 12 classes, many of them handled classes, so we put on a mixture of Gurnays and show pigeons. After entering two in every class we had three show birds left in the basket when we came to the last class. Joe said, 'Put those back in the van, it is only a wire class.' I told him 'No, we will put them in, you never know what fool will judge the wires class as they have a separate judge for most classes.'

We won nine classes out of the first 11 and we then went upstairs to collect our birds and find out who had won the last class, the wires class. An old man came down the stairs carrying a small basket covered in dirt, with two pigeons in. I asked him, 'Who won the wires class?' He replied 'That chap with those like ducks; first, second and third.' (Ours for sure!) Joe turned on him and said, 'Where do you come from?' 'Todmorden' was the reply. Joe responded by saying, 'Then when you get to the bottom of the stairs throw that mucky basket and those two birds in the canal and if they fail to float to Todmorden you are better without them!'

When we returned over Cockhill it started a few flakes of snow but we were the two happiest lads in England!!

Jean had trained as a baker on leaving school, but had not returned to it after the war. But she was, and still is, a very good baker. One day, Joe saw some of the cakes and buns, etc. that Jean had produced and said that we'd show some of them in the next agricultural show.

So for the next three years we continued to show both pigeons and Jean's baking. The prize money at this time was £1 for a first, 15/- for second and 10/- for a third in both pigeons and baking. We went round all the shows in West Yorkshire and, on average, won about three firsts with pigeons and the same with the baking, plus the usual seconds and thirds. This was every Saturday that we could find a show.

We were then receiving more than a week's wage in prize money, which Joe and myself shared between us. Though also we had our laughs along the way.

1959 was one of the hottest summers for years and at Pudsey Show in midsummer the heat was appalling, We entered some coconut buns that Jean had made, turned them upside down so that they looked just like pyramids. I entered them on a nice doyley on a green table covering and, as they looked very different, I thought they could win. After the judging I went to see what we had won, these coconut pyramids had first prize on them. I went back into the pigeon marquee until the show was about over, before returning to collect Jean's baking. Two farmers' wives were looking at the remains of the pyramids, which had melted with the heat, but still had the first-prize card on them. One lady said, 'I could do better than that myself.' The other lady replied, 'Yes they remind me of a BLOODY COW CLAP!!'

We then continued round the summer shows each year, starting with the first show at Otley and the last one at Pateley Bridge, that being the last of the summer shows.

We won at Otley one year, and then went to Wetherby on the Tuesday of the following week and won the cup for best in show. The pigeon that won at Otley got nothing at Wetherby, and the one that won the cup at Wetherby got nothing at Otley. It also happened to be the same judge; so much for his ability to recognise pigeons!

Now sometime in late summer, we entered the pigeons and the usual baking at a show in Mirfield. Though on this day, for some reason, Joe could not go with me, and as Jean was open in the shop on a Saturday, I had to go on my own.

Just before I continue this story, let me tell you that as well as the shop being open on Saturday, we opened on a Sunday and all weekdays as well. We got as well known as the Windmill Theatre in London did during the war. We got the same motto: WE NEVER CLOSE!

On getting to Mirfield I placed all baking in each class as usual, and then the pigeons in the other tent close by. After the show was over and almost closing I went to see what we had won in the baking section. Jean had entered six tarts, three jam and three lemon, and they had won first prize.

We had other prizes as well, but an old lady was looking longingly at these tarts when she said to me, 'Are these yours?' I said, 'Yes.' She replied, 'Will you sell me them, they are a lot better than any I can get in the shops.' I said to her, 'Yes, but I have to go into the pigeon tent so help yourself and give me what you think they are worth, as I have no idea of the price.'

Being longer than I expected with the pigeons, I was returning to the bakery tent not caring if the lady paid or not as we did not ourselves eat the produce in case cigarette ash had been dropped into them; we used to feed the poultry or dog with them.

Now just as I was about to enter the tent the old lady came out waving a ten-shilling note. I was just about to say I had no change when she said to me, 'Here you are, tarts are 2s/6d a dozen at home and I have bought four dozen so that is right.' She ran off saying something about a bus to catch.

I then realised I had sold everyone else's entries in the tart class!

After collecting my other entries and prize cards I was on my way home rather quickly!

Another big show we decided to enter was at Bridlington. Four of us went to this show, Joe, myself and a chap called John Lister and another man, Tommy Crabtree. Tommy and myself had set clocks together many times and we used to set clocks at times for Harrogate federation at the County Hotel on the Stray, as well as our own club and federation. The reason we used to go to Harrogate is that it was a paid job in those days.

Because it was a special race they used independent clock setters. I think it should still be so today, as pigeon racing is very competitive and it would appear fairer to everyone.

Now back to the Bridlington trip. We took about 20 birds and as the show had ten or so classes, we entered all of them. Then we all went into town and had a pub lunch, after buying some raffle tickets.

When we returned to the show at about 2.00pm, we had won most of the classes plus many seconds and thirds; in fact, it was a field day! Joe organised the packing up of the birds with John, while Tommy and myself collected the cards and went to the secretary to collect our winnings. Joe then shouted in the door, 'We are ready to go.' The secretary then said, 'Just a minute, you lot have won five tins of biscuits in the Christmas raffle!' So when we finally got ready to go, the secretary said to us, 'Take care on your way home, I know you come from near Ilkley Moor Bah't 'at and thanks again for coming but please DON'T COME AGAIN!!'

While writing about Tommy Crabtree, my old friend from Clock Setting Days, let me tell you this true story about Tommy.

Before he worked as the boilerman at the Low Mill in Addingham, he was a farm labourer in the Langbar area. One day, he was sent to collect 13 young cows from the goods yard at Ilkley station. This was before the present amount of traffic was on the roads and in the days when everything came by rail.

His journey was down Brook Street and then NEW Brook Street and by the back roads to Langbar. This was before the Wheatsheaf Hotel at the end of Church Street and New Brook Street was pulled down.

On his way down Brook Street, 12 of the cows carried on down the road but one cow went through the front door of the Wheatsheaf, which was open, straight through the passage and out of the back door and rejoined the others.

When Tommy got to the door he just had a look through the front door, but did not go in and no one seemed to be around. This cow had messed as it went in and flicked its tail around and cow muck was all up the walls and some was even hanging from the CEILING!

TOMMY KEPT ON WALKING.

Before the previous event I almost had a worse disaster, again at Mirfield. I was the one who did all the clerical work to do with the shows, obtaining both the schedules and doing all the entering for both the pigeons and the baking.

At Mirfield this particular year, I made a mistake in the entries and when the receipt of entry slips came back, I had put something on the wrong line and of all things, I entered the JAR OF PICKLED ONIONS.

These I had not a clue about and Jean and Joe both had their say about my lack of efficiency! So a few days later I went into the Co-op in Addingham and asked the manager, who happened to come to serve me (no self-service in those days), if I could buy three jars of pickled onions, but I wanted to come round the back and select my own. He said, 'You always have to be different,' and then allowed me to select my own.

I took the three jars home and emptied the lot into one of Jean's large baking bowls, washed the label from one of the jars and then put back in this jar all the nice round ones that appeared to be the same size.

Then I put on this jar one of my own labels I had made with 'Pickled Onions 1959' on it. Jean and Joe said this would be thrown out of the show! Nevertheless, I took it myself, and after judging, went into the tent to see that I had won first prize with this exhibit.

When going up to the table, this fancy lady was saying, 'Who's Jean Holmes, I have won the onions for the last ten years?' I stood behind her and replied in a light squeaky voice, 'I am my dear!' She grabbed her onions and ran out of the tent as she thought I was a bit queer.

One of the last items we took round the shows in 1962, before Joe and myself had to give it up as we both got too busy in each of our own businesses, was a blue twinset. This fine blue twinset had little white rabbits round the bottom and had been knitted for little Shirley, who was then nearly four years old.

We started showing this garment in the early shows and it won first every time we entered it. So it was far too valuable for us to let Shirley wear it, even though she kept asking, 'When can I wear my twinset?' Our reply was always the same, 'Next week!'

By the beginning of August, Jean said we were going to have to let her wear it soon or it would be too small for her. So we agreed that she could do so after the Bingley Show in August.

Joe and myself went to Bingley with the pigeons and the usual list of baking, plus the twinset. In the afternoon I went from the pigeon tent to see how we had got on in the baking tent. On returning to Joe in the pigeons, he asked how much we had won. I replied, telling him all about the baking, then added, 'and second with the twinset.' 'What beat the twinset?' was his reply. I said I had not bothered to look as the tent was full of women. Joe then said, 'Come on we must see what got first in front of us.' We had a job to find the winner, but when we did it was at the far end of the tent. Joe and myself looked and saw it was a pair of men's socks, that Joe would have accepted except the feet were about 18 inches long and the legs only six inches long. Joe said aloud, 'Who knit those things!' An old lady of about five foot tall was stood in front of them and replied, 'I did, for my husband Archie.' Now he was only about 4'8" tall and was stood in front of her and we had not seen him. Joe then said to her, 'You are not married to him are you, because the size of the feet on those socks, I was sure you had married KING KONG.' He had the place in uproar and the stewards and judge were nowhere to be found!

Yes, we had a great three years and proved that we could make 'Showing for Profit' a success, but what was more important, it was fun, fun and FUN all the way, I would not have missed it for the WORLD!!

THE FIRST FOUR YEARS
IN BUSINESS

In 1962, Jean got so busy in the shop and I had left the railway by then, so I joined her full time, and from then on we made a great effort to get more trade for the shop. This we soon achieved and much of this trade came from the Bolton Abbey area and my many friends I had known for years. Some of these had been family friends and others from my cricket-playing days.

I was asked the previous year if I would play again for Bolton Abbey cricket club, and this I agreed to do. It was a much younger side than the 1947 side but still had some players who had played for years, to name a few: Roger and Leonard Tiffany, Tony and Michael Curtis, John Verity and still one or two of the 1947 side: John Hartley, Herbert Holmes and Ken and Keith Newall.

The summer of 1962 must have been a fine and dry summer because I opened the batting again but this time with Roger Tiffany as my partner. In this year, 1962, I broke the club record for most runs scored in one season. I made 845 runs. This was playing Saturdays only, no Sunday cricket then, and the odd game at Whitsuntide and bank holiday. I was presented with a small cup for this performance, but thought nothing of it at the time. Now, looking back, it must have been well out of the ordinary because, to the best of my knowledge, this record has stood for over 35 years.

Now, in this year, tragedy struck Uncle Fred. He had to have part of his leg amputated because of bad circulation problems. He was now almost 80 years of age and I went every night for the next three years to help him upstairs to bed, until he died.

For all of this setback he used to tell me all of his poaching activities, from around the time of the First World War.

Though not to be outdone, Aunt Eva told me this about him. He invited her to his home to stay the weekend with Fred's parents before they got married.

Eva being a farmer's daughter thought she would help future mother-in-law to butter the bread for Saturday tea. On going into the large bread pots that were used for home-baked bread in those days, she put the lid back on the first of these pots QUICKLY, as inside were two live cock chickens! Then, for Sunday lunch, she also noticed they had chicken!!

Asking Fred about this later, he replied, 'I sent Allan (my father) out to get two chickens from some hen hut, but I thought he would have had sense to pluck them ready for the oven!'

Full marks to Eva after that start, she still married him, but she did say, 'At least he had seven keys for property in Addingham to rent on the day he asked me to marry him!'

Together, they lived in around 27 different houses in Addingham, all of them to rent in those days. They even moved to the house next door in 'Daisy Hill' and 'Crag View', as the houses next door had been newly decorated!

When my father was a young man he got caught poaching in the fields across the road from Chelker Reservoir. This was rough land then and not the farmland that it is today. He had to appear in Skipton court, where the gamekeeper told the court he had seen him go past a CORN STACK and had recognised my father from about 200 yards away.

My father's representative objected to this statement, saying there were no CORN STACKS in this part of Yorkshire and if he could not see this was a HAYSTACK how could he tell my father from that distance. He then produced another man to stand next to my father and asked the court if they could tell the difference at 200 yards.

The magistrate was old and looked over his glasses and said, 'I cannot tell the difference at ten yards, CASE DISMISSED!'

You see, my grandfather and Fred hired an Irish labourer who was available at the Swan looking for work. These men came every year looking for work, they dressed him up in some of my father's clothes and they picked someone who could have been his twin; all it cost them was a couple of pounds!

A gamekeeper at another time was always around the Addingham end of the Duke of Devonshire's estate, and was becoming a big problem to the poachers trying to feed their families. However, on this day, about six of them, including Fred and my father, all had a day out.

In this day, the only sort of day out you could go to, you had to walk.

So it was decided the venue would be Appletreewick.

They all followed the footpath by the river up to Appletreewick and then spent some time in the New Inn and the Craven Arms playing darts and dominoes. This must have been in early summer because they stayed late and started to walk home when the new moon came up, and this was almost half full. Poachers and moons go together.

Walking home on the road, when getting below the Strid Woods, they saw in the moonlight all the same gamekeeper's pheasant pens, in which he was rearing young pheasants for the October 1st shooting season. They went over the wall and just opened all the pen doors and then carried on home.

Of course, next morning at daybreak, all the young pheasants, only the size of small chicks, would run into the woods and escape only to be eaten by foxes and vermin and certainly could not be caught. The gamekeeper would have to report to the estate office that he had lost hundreds or all of the pheasants, so he was sacked or he left within the next two weeks, so yet another problem was solved!

Many years before, Fred worked for the local doctor and they both had to turn out on horseback if they received a call during the night for the. Fred went on a separate horse to the doctor, so that if the patient had to be taken to the hospital, Fred would borrow a local farmer's cart and take the ill person to hospital with his horse and then return with the empty cart. This would then allow the doctor to go home or to the next call.

One day, when being called to someone near the Strid at Bolton Abbey, a local man, I think called Mr Roberts, said to Fred and the doctor, 'I will not call you two out when I am dying, I will throw myself in the Strid and end it all!' Several years later, there was a search out for Mr Roberts, he was missing from home and could not be found.

Fred then said to the doctor, 'Do you remember him telling us he would end his life in the river, you don't think he has done do you doctor?' Doctor: 'Probably, you never know.' About three weeks later, his body was found in the river!

A well-known man, who worked in the woods on the Bolton Abbey estate, met Fred in the pub in Addingham the day after the body was recovered. The man from Bolton Abbey was also a well-known fish poacher and would fish in his lunch hour and then put his rod up a hollow tree until the next lunchtime. He would sell the fish in Addingham for his profit.

So on the day Mr Robert's body was recovered, he said to Fred he was pleased he had been found as for the last fortnight he was the only one who knew his whereabouts as he had seen him on the bed of the river a fortnight ago, while casting for fish, but did not report it for fear of being caught poaching fish, as he had no permission to be in the area at all.

It has been a long fortnight waiting for someone to recover the body and seeing I was the last to see him alive and dead I will have to attend his funeral!

Now into the start of 1964, I was delivering to a lady in a bungalow at the corner of Springfield Mount and Bolton Road. She told me that they would be moving to Guernsey the following September; her husband was not in good health. He was a plumber by trade and had got a job there in the greenhouses; he hoped his health would improve in that climate.

In the shop, we were getting very short of space for the three of us and all the stock we had to hold. So I asked the lady if I could bring Jean to see this house some evening as we could be interested in buying another property. She said bring her tonight, and I knew that Jean would be sure to like this house the moment she saw it.

I was not wrong, in fact she was delighted with it.

We bought this house, in fact it was really a dormer bungalow, in March, and said the lady could stay in it until the September. Our intention was to run the shop and live in this bungalow, this is what we started to do. By now, Shirley had started at school and for the first few months stayed for lunch and was happy.

When we moved into the bungalow, Jean and myself had a change of plan. We decided to rent the shop and house on lease for a period of ten years and then when Shirley was older she would always have something behind her to start her own life.

In the meantime, I saw a man called Bert Robinson, who told me about a vacant job as reservoir keeper at Chelker Reservoir working for Bradford Corporation Water Works.

I rang Bradford about this job and was told to go for an interview at the office in George Street, Bradford. When I arrived for interview I was shown into the deputy engineer's office.

He and another man present asked me all about my past employment, etc., then said, 'Do you know the area?' I told them the name of every field and who farmed it from Barden to Silsden Moor. They were very impressed, and said I was the man they were looking for.

I could have told them every rabbit hole as well, but I kept that to myself.

I got the job, and started in September 1964. Jean was now at home and I thought life could not be better, and so ended the 'First Four Years in Business.'

CHELKER IN ALL WEATHERS

I started work at Chelker Reservoir and I really liked the outdoor life. There were two men working under me, one was Bert Robinson who told me about the job, but he was nearing retirement and did not work long with me before he did retire. The other man was Harry Hudson, the same man who I helped up the steps from the river in the flood in 1936, some 30 years before. Now Harry and I got on very well together as he had been a poacher all his life and of course I had done my fair share.

Jean was now at home, in the bungalow, which we had named 'Fairholme' as it had no name at the time we bought it, having been built only a few years earlier.

I thought Jean would see to Shirley and get her to school and everyone would be happy. How wrong can you be?! She would no way go to school if Jean was at home, although she had gone perfectly the year before, when Jean was working in the shop. Shirley made all the excuses under the sun for not going, like Jean had to do no baking without her, or play on her swing, and a thousand other reasons!

Jean got so upset at her crying buckets full of tears that she could not push her through the school gates. So that job fell to me and I shut the school gates behind her every morning for the next few months. I used to have to ring the waterworks at 9.00 am every morning from home, so it worked perfectly for me to push her into school then go back home and ring the office and have a coffee! I really needed it!!

I used to ring the office again just before 4.00 pm, in case any extra water was required at Bradford, so I could pick Shirley up from school on my way home. In the evening, Shirley had such a lovely smile when she came out of school and was a real treasure to be with. Though in the morning I could gladly have disowned her!

Now when I bought the shop at 143 Main Street, my old school master from Addingham junior school told me that I was doing the 'wrong thing' in buying the shop! This annoyed me, as I did not get on with him at school, nor did I ask for his advice as I never thought he had much tact and was in no way suitable to be in business.

When I bought 'Fairholme' he lived in an old semi on the same road. One day he was passing our house, when I said to him, 'Do you now think I have done the wrong thing? I own two houses and the shop in the village and have just bought this bungalow all in four years!' He went on his way without reply.

I had waited over 20 years to get my own back!!

At Chelker Reservoir my job was to walk the pipe track from below Barden reservoir to Bolton Abbey below the station, then over Haw Pike Farm top and to the valve house below Chelker Reservoir. Then on past Sanfit farms and over the Silsden road from Addingham and up to the valve house at almost the top of Brown Bank road, Silsden. The distance would be well over seven miles and over some of the worst territory of the Yorkshire Dales, It could blow a gale on those hilltops from September to June.

We used to have a saying when setting off to walk the pipe track, 'Take your mac if it's fine, please yourself if it's raining!'

When Bert Robinson retired, it was not long before Eddie Hudson, Harry's younger brother, applied for the vacant job. I set him on to work with us and the three of us had a very happy eight years or so together. Later I will explain how Eddie and myself worked together for several more years in a totally different job.

Jean had by now, in early 1965, got pretty fed up with Shirley's antics about not going to school that she thought about going out to work again. So when an advert appeared the following week in the Craven Herald for a lady to be manageress for the well-known shop Whitakers Chocolatiers in the High Street, Skipton, Jean phoned the shop and went for an interview, only to return home to inform me that she had got the job and would start the following week! My heart sank, not because I thought Jean could not do the job, but how would I manage this despicable child!!

Though manage I did, because the day Jean went out to work again, Shirley was transformed into a lovely little girl and never cried or played up again.

The only time I was none too pleased with her was years later when she went to school on her own. One night I was late home, only by about 20 minutes because I had to repair a burst on one of the local farms that we supplied water to. When I got home I found Shirley sat on the front step, crying. I had previously told her that if I should at any time be late, to go in next door to Barbara who Shirley visited every day and wait there until I got home. So I said to Shirley, 'Stop crying and wipe your eyes, you should have gone to Barbara's as I told you.' All Shirley said was, 'I was waiting for you.' With that settled I forgot all about it, that was until approximately six months later, when, with Jean, I went to a parents' evening at her school. At the end of one paper on her home she had put in large letters, AND MY FATHER IS <u>ALWAYS </u>LOCKING ME <u>OUT</u>!! Once in her whole lifetime and she reported me!!

The house 'Fairholme' had a large garden including five lawns, so with Jean working I spent most of my spare time in the garden. One day, I was making a base for a greenhouse when the owner of the field behind the house came to the garden fence to chat to me. His name was Jack Dixon (senior), who I had known all my life. He was an old man by this time and had been retired many years. Jack asked me if I was making a base for a pigeon loft as we had both flown pigeons many years in both Silsden and Addingham pigeon clubs. He had a loft of about 60 pigeons at the bottom of the field below our back garden.

He then informed me that he hoped I was going to build a loft again as he was now too old to come from home every day and look after the birds. He then said he was going to give me all his birds if I would feed them and see to them, and that I could race them to his loft.

I thanked him for his very generous offer, but said I would only be able to do it if he would sell me a strip of land from the field next to my boundary fence, so that I could put a loft on my own land for future use. We agreed on this deal and he said he would make the full agreement, so we shook hands, and he said, 'See to the pigeons from tomorrow Bob, I am very poorly.' Jack unfortunately went into hospital on the Tuesday or Wednesday, so

I never spoke to him again. I got a great shock when informed he had died on the Friday morning.

Jean and I then decided a few days after the funeral we would go and see Jack's widow and explain the talk I had with Jack and see if she knew anything about our agreement, because we could confirm nothing about it as we had nothing in writing.

Now Jack's widow was his second wife (his first had died many years earlier), who was previously Miss Alice Dinsdale, who Jean had worked for at her bakehouse shop after leaving school to learn the baking trade.

We went to see Alice and after welcoming us into her house she at once said I know you are here about the land and pigeons, Jack told me about it all and now everything has still to go on as agreed and that she would make all the arrangements.

Jean and I were very pleased with this, it made all the difference to the back of our property. We soon got the new fence up and built a new pigeon loft to go on it. It also turned out that I then flew pigeons to this loft for a further eight years, and with great success.

The pipe track past Chelker Reservoir takes water in two thirty-six-inch pipes to Bradford. This water comes from Scar House reservoir at the top end of Nidderdale. While I was at Chelker for those eight years, we put another 42-inch pipe alongside the other two so that for very many years to come Bradford should never be without water. Now, from Barden reservoir to Chelker Reservoir and then on to Bradford is a much older tunnel that took the original water supply to Bradford. This was built in 1858 and is still in use today.

From Chelker, at the Draughton end of the reservoir, is the tower from which you open a valve to let further water from Chelker into this tunnel. On a summer day in about 1967, it was decided that this tunnel required inspecting for any potential blockages. Harry Hudson and myself were asked if we would do the job as not many men from Bradford or the engineers fancied it, as the tunnel goes right under Chelker Reservoir. After the water had been turned off at Barden Reservoir the day before, Harry and myself entered the tunnel in the field to the Draughton end of the reservoir by way of a 12-foot ladder. We had waist waders on plus tin helmets and two lights each. You have to walk slightly bent forward as the tunnel is only about five feet three inches high in certain areas. It is about four feet wide and dug out from solid rock, with no lining and a rough floor. In many places you can see the pick marks where the men cut the tunnel before 1858. The walk takes you down the far side of the reservoir to the air shaft that you can see as a round tower in a small field across the reservoir. You now realise how far underground you are, as when you look up all you see is a faint glimmer of light. On we went, right under the reservoir, and the next light you see is when looking up the air shaft on the road side, so now you know you are clear of the reservoir but still with half a mile to go to complete the trip. This ends when you get to the old reservoir in Heathness Ghyll. You climb out up a short ladder of about three yards. Now that was over 30 years ago and to this day I do not know any man who has walked UNDER Chelker Reservoir.

On another occasion, during a very hard, frosty winter, I was told to turn on more water from the tower at Chelker Reservoir. The tower gets covered in ice in an east wind, to turn on any water I had to walk on the tower platform with nothing to hold on to, with a drop on each side into 37 feet of ice-cold water, alone and very dangerous. One day, when requested to turn on extra water, I was not prepared to risk my life on the platform. In any case, I knew the valve would be frozen solid. So I took a photograph of the platform complete with all the ice on it, and forwarded it to the engineer's office in Bradford, saying if water was that urgent someone would have to come through and assist. I never heard another word. Though a few years later, when going into the entrance hall of the head office in George Street, Bradford, someone had blown up my small photograph and there it hung on the wall; the caption read 'Chelker in all weathers.'

During the mid-to-late sixties I got an invitation to judge at the Birmingham Mail International Pigeon Show at Bingley Hall, Birmingham. This was one of the largest shows in England for this period of time. It was sponsored by the Birmingham Mail newspaper, who arranged everything including our rail travel and hotel accommodation in a first-class hotel in New Street, Birmingham.

On arrival at the hotel we were introduced to the officials of the newspaper and the show officials, plus other judges, about 24 of them, and we all stayed together for dinner on the two days for which the show lasted.

We were all taken to the show on the morning, each of the judges then being introduced to his own steward who was with him for the rest of the show. We were then given our judging book and on looking at this, I found I was to judge the class 75 Mile Young Hens. Checking the pen numbers for this class, I found that there were 88 pigeons entered in this class.

Ice breaking on Chelker, 1965.

'Chelker in all weathers.'

After I had completed my task and selected those that had won a prize card, eight cards per class, I thought the hen I placed first was a very nice young hen indeed. The steward then took the judging book to the show secretary, and both of us had the lunch that had been provided.

During the time we were having our lunch, another judge stayed behind to judge the 25 class winners, to award the 'Best in show' and the 'Best opposite sex'.

After returning back into the hall after lunch, I found that the young hen I had selected had won the 'Best opposite sex award'. Many of my fellow judges congratulated me for picking the second-best bird in almost 3000 birds. I was a very proud man indeed at this my first international show, as the standard at this level is extremely high.

I came home and continued to race and show my own few birds, thinking that judging at Birmingham was to be the highlight of my pigeon career.

Yet only two years later I was shocked and surprised to receive another invitation to judge at Birmingham Mail. Many people never have the chance to judge at these shows once in their lives, yet to have been selected twice was to me an honour indeed.

Again at Birmingham it was the same procedure, hotel at night and judging the next morning. This time, the class I had to judge was 200 mile old hens. This was a very big class of 108 entries, with some very high-class, good pigeons entered. I finally selected for first prize a fine-looking dark white flight hen.

Going back into the hall after lunch, I really was shocked to see this bird had been awarded the 'Best opposite sex'. To have done this once was to make me proud enough, but twice I can only say I was over the moon. I continued to race my pigeons at home with considerable success, and from time to time I was asked to donate a pigeon for the various charity sales taking place around the country. One day, I received a letter asking me if I would donate a pigeon to a charity sale about to take place in America on behalf of a nurses' organisation. This I agreed to do and my pigeon, a fine dark cock with one white flight in each wing, was sent from London to America with about another 150 pigeons.

The sale of these pigeons was held on television in the city of Philadelphia. It was several months before I saw a report on the sale of these pigeons. But when I did finally see one I was very pleased, for the pigeon I had donated had made the third-highest price in the sale.

Now I had a very successful period from 1965 to 1969, racing to my loft at the bungalow. This was recognised by many pigeon fanciers, but none more so than by Thomas L. Smith, jnr, of the USA, who wrote a fine article about me, including a photograph of myself, the loft and a winning pigeon, in the Racing Pigeon Bulletin of America on August 24th 1970. When he published this article its title was 'Methods of the Masters'.

I know many people will have won more than me in five years, but what pleased me most of all was the final words of my success and I quote. 'What is even more impressive is that he sent an average of only seven birds per race!'

RETURN TO BUSINESS

In early 1971 Jean and I were thinking of going back into business in the shop as the lease would expire in just over 20 months' time.

My mother, who was still living next door to the shop, at 145 Main Street, Addingham, was taken very ill and she died on March 15th 1971. We then owned 145 Main Street but kept it empty as we then wished to make a big house from the two cottages, 145 and 143. This would create much more space behind the shop, as this had been a major problem during our first four years there.

During the summer of 1971, we thought the shop business was not doing very well and also the people in it were not in the best of health. Thinking they may wish to leave before their lease expired, we thought it best if we moved into the cottage, 145 Main Street, in preparation for the further move into the shop premises when they became vacant.

We decided to try and sell our bungalow, 'Fairholme', during the summer. We told some of our relatives about this prior to officially putting it on the market through an estate agent. Two of our relatives appeared a little interested and asked us the price, we replied £6,000.

After a time, they appeared not to want to buy it, and Jean and I decided we would wait a few more weeks before putting it in the hands of the estate agent.

Within a day or so of this, a man Jean knew from when she worked in Ilkley came walking past our bungalow to look at another that was for sale on the same road. He stopped and spoke to Jean and said he would much prefer to buy our bungalow rather than the one he had looked at, if it was for sale. Jean told him to come in and have a look round as we were going to sell shortly. It was ideal and just what he was looking for, but how much was our asking price? I said £7,000, to which he said he would have it there and then. So we sold the bungalow and moved back to 145, next door to the shop, in late 1971.

We then had a surprise before Christmas: the tenants of the shop were not well and would like to leave the shop, even though there was almost one and a half years of the lease still to run.

We agreed we would let them leave in early January, after they sold their Christmas stock. We started trading in January 1972 and Jean got so busy within weeks that I had to leave my job at Chelker to help her.

I could not serve in the shop at first as in the previous year, 1971, decimalisation had taken place. Jean had got used to it but being at Chelker I had never used money, so Jean had to teach me the new coins before I could serve.

We broke through the wall between the two downstairs rooms of 143 and 145 and made one big house. This gave us all the extra room we had always needed. We then divided a room to create a bathroom and a storeroom, allowing us to increase our stock by at least twice.

This year, we continued to get more business every week and we were now delivering goods to all parts of the district, from Silsden Moor, to Burnsall and Blubberhouses.

I met the tenant of another grocer's shop, 146 Main Street, which was on the other side of the street to ours. This man was approaching retirement age and it was well known that his wife was not in very good health. We were in a wholesale warehouse in Keighley when I started talking to him, and he said he would like to get out of his shop if he could find someone to buy his stock. I agreed to buy the stock from him if he could get me the tenancy of the property.

He came to see me a few days later to say he had arranged for me to see his landlord with a view to renting his property, and if I could agree suitable terms, then he would sell out to me.

Jean and I went to see the owner of this property, a farmer's wife from Spofforth, near Harrogate. She was a nice lady, much older than us, and when I told her my name, she asked if I was any relation of Allan Holmes, to which I replied he was my late father. She appeared as shocked as I was at this coincidence, as she had rented property to my father many years before.

*Addingham Gala
'Shirley goes to Ascot.'*

*Christmas
Exhibition,
1977, in
Addingham
Memorial Hall*

We took out the lease on this property for the following eight years. We now owned two shops and more business was coming our way every week. Being open seven days a week in one shop and six days in the other, we needed to take on more staff. Jean had to manage both shops and took on day staff, Saturday staff and Sunday girls.

I was now far too busy to serve on a lot: working behind the scenes, going to Bradford market most mornings by 5.00 am, then delivering orders part of the day. Also, I had to see all the travellers that came for orders, as most wholesale firms made deliveries direct if you required a substantial amount, and we always did.

We had an exhibition in the Memorial Hall before each Christmas and many of our customers came from miles around to select and order Christmas goods to be delivered at the appropriate time. Jean and I by now had so little time to speak to each other during the day that many evenings we used to trip on to the Devonshire Arms Hotel at Bolton Abbey for dinner, just to be on our own to discuss staffing arrangements and other business ideas without interruptions.

These visits made us very good friends with the Hodgson family and staff, and in turn brought us yet again more business to our two shops. Whenever the hotel was short of some kind of grocery, we always came to their rescue.

The previous tenants of the shop had started to sell Sunday newspapers (not any weekday ones). This brought extra trade for us on a Sunday, bringing in more people who often picked up other things as well as the papers.

One day, the wholesale agent for Sunday papers, who was an Addingham lad and had gone to the same junior school as I had done, came to ask me if I would take over the whole of the retail area from Silsden Moor to Burnsall, Appletreewick, Bolton Abbey and all the places in between, as well as what we already did, the whole of Addingham. This gave us a chance of another business as a sideline, so we took it on as it was a monopoly trade and no one could sell papers in your area.

I asked my friend from Chelker days, Eddie Hudson, to help me with this project, which he did. We delivered papers in the van together for the next ten years. In fact, we never missed a Sunday in all that time for holidays, ill health or anything else, not even adverse weather conditions, a record of which I am still proud today. With regard to the weather conditions in the Dales, we only seemed to get wet through about a dozen times in all that time, so much so that a lady in Addingham did her washing between eight and 11 on a Sunday morning. She said it never rained and that someone was looking after those two up the Dales.

We had our laughs along the way, the very first streaker to be shown in the Sunday newspaper was the man who ran on to the rugby pitch at Twickenham and was taken off the pitch by two police officers, with one of the officers holding his helmet to cover the man up. This picture was on the front page of the News of the World. On this day, Eddie was to deliver these papers and did not like suggestive things put in the newspapers. I told him we only deliver them, not print them, so no one can blame you for the contents or photographs shown. He continued to deliver the papers, but still complained about this photo on the front page. When he then got to a house that had been converted from a barn, just east of Burnsall, he stood at the door holding this paper with the photo on the front, having rung the door bell, and with the house having a stone floor he could hear the lady almost at the door. At this exact moment the belt on his trousers broke and at the very same time the zip on his fly broke and his trousers fell round his knees.

The door then opened and the lady saw him standing there with this photo in one hand and him holding his trousers between his legs with the other.

She at once thought he was being very rude and grabbed the paper from him, gave him the money, then banged the door in his face!

He got back in the van and I could not stop laughing at him, when he turned to me and said that the lady could have asked me what was the matter, I was only going to ask her for a piece of string!!

Dogs, of course, we had plenty of trouble with over the years. One in particular that I remember was a real villain. No barking to warn you of his presence, just a quick nip at your ankle if you were not on your guard. The house was in Appletreewick and had a long path up to the front door with lawns on either side and a privet hedge on each side beyond the lawn. This dog, a Jack Russell called Bonzo, would wait under the hedge then make a dash over the lawn, make a bite for your ankle and tear away under the opposite hedge. If it failed to get you on the way to the house, it sure got you on the way back.

One day, on the way back to the van, the dog got Eddie through his trousers and sock; blood was pouring from his ankle. We had some plasters in the van, carried out the necessary first aid and then continued on with the rest of the round.

The next week, when we arrived at this same house, Eddie said I shall get that dog today if it attacks me. Now Eddie had been a good footballer in his day; he played left back, and not many players got past Eddie with the ball. So I was expecting fireworks as he set off up the path.

About halfway up the path, this dog came charging out from under the privet hedge, but Eddie was more than ready for it and half turned, and with his famous left foot, lifted the dog at least eight feet into the air. It had done a couple of somersaults before it landed in the middle of one of the lawns. When it crashed to the ground it just lay there, slowly shaking its head and looking at Eddie. It very slowly started to wag its short tail, when, at this precise moment, the lady of the house opened the door. Whilst I was sure that she had seen her dog in the air and we would get the sack, she turned to Eddie and in such a sweet voice, said, 'I do believe that at last Bonzo has taken a FANCY TO YOU!'

When delivering on Sunday mornings, many people were still in bed, so from time to time we had to leave them a note inside the paper to inform them how much was due, and everyone was good enough to pay their accounts the following week.

Travelling along one day, Eddie was looking at the account book and making a bill out for the next call at a house called 'Ivy Cottage'. He asked me, 'What do they call the man at Ivy Cottage?' I replied, 'I have no idea, you always deliver that house.' Eddie then said, 'I seem to remember something about a Mr Johnson, I will put that down, it's near enough.' He then delivered the papers with the note enclosed.

On arriving at this house the following week, this man was stood on the step waiting for us in his pyjamas. He looked a right sight, a little man with an extra-long neck, which his too-small pyjamas made look even worse. At his feet was a long sausage dog that had an even longer neck and looked really miserable. The pair looked as though they were from a comedy film.

Anyway, Eddie gave him the papers and the man paid him for the bill enclosed the previous week. Eddie was about to turn to get back in the van when the man said, 'By the way, my name is not Mr Johnson, that is the name of my dog.' Eddie stood in disbelief, saying, 'I beg your pardon.' The man repeated that Mr Johnson was the name of his dog. Eddie replied, 'I have never heard of a dog called Mr Johnson, never ever, so what do I call you on next month's bill, FIDO?'

I used to deliver all the papers in the Red Lion, Burnsall, to the owner, staff and all the guests staying overnight. While I was busy in the Red Lion, I parked the van outside and Eddie, to save time, made deliveries to the cottages in the village. That was except one at the top of the street above the Red Lion. An old man who we thought would be about 80 always asked every Sunday how we thought stocks and shares were doing. Eddie would not go to this house, as he said he knew nothing about shares. I knew even less, but each time I delivered I made up some tale about a poor crop of coffee beans so prices should go up, trouble in Palestine so oil could go up. I thought of a different story each week. When I asked him which papers he wanted, he thanked me for my information, smiled and said one of everything. He got about nine papers in all, gave me two pounds, often much more and said keep the change. I had to keep up these tales as I could not do without customers as good as this.

One day, Eddie said he would go for some reason; I think I had been delayed in the Red Lion. I followed up in the van, when Eddie knocked on the door. The door opened and on the step stood this well-made girl of about 19 in a bright pink babydoll nightie. This nightie had been washed and no doubt shrunk or she could have developed since she had bought it, because from the van I could see it only covered a small part of her, most of it the wrong parts.

Now Eddie was slightly cross-eyed, with one eye at 11 o'clock and one at three. No one took any notice of this, but when he got excited both eyes revolved in opposite directions. At this point in time it looked to this girl as if he was going into ORBIT! She stood looking at Eddie and wondered what he was looking at. I could see from the van it was not the nightie. She then said, 'Do you like it?', and gave him a twirl on the doorstep. He then at long last got the papers delivered and into the van. He said, 'Did you see that cheeky young miss?' I was still laughing and said, 'Yes.' Eddie replied, 'You will never see that old man again if that cheeky miss is looking after him.' The end to this story is we never did see the old man again!

We have now got well into the late seventies and the shops were really busy.

One day, a lady parked her car facing Ilkley, and came across the road into the shop. Jean went into the shop and for some reason I followed behind, probably to check some stock, as I never interfered with Jean serving customers. Then, while in the shop, I just glanced across the road at this lady's car and it was moving down the street with no one in it, not even a driver.

I had no chance to reach the shop door in time, so I ran through the house, 143, and through the house, 145, out of the end door and down the footpath after the car travelling towards Ilkley. Luckily no cars were coming from Ilkley, so I ran further down the white line in the middle of the road as fast as I could. I caught up with the car by The Fleece Inn, and still running, managed to open the driver's door and with a great leap, jumped into the driver's seat and brought the car to a halt by the end of the car park. Getting out, I leaned on the car as I had not run so hard and fast for years. Many people had come out by our shops to see what had happened. I was still leaning on the car, out of breath and still suffering from the shock, when I just glanced in the back of the car and there was a small baby in the back seat just smiling up at me.

In 1978, Shirley got engaged to her boyfriend with a view to getting married in February 1980. He was a farmer living in Glusburn, and they bought a cottage in the village near the family farm of Town End.

Shirley left the business and took up residence in Glusburn working on the farm, doing the milk round and still continuing her training to be a further-education teacher in the field of fashion.

This left us with a difficult decision to make: how long were we going to continue in business now it was clear that Shirley would not take over from us, as we had once hoped. Jean and I had then to decide whether we wished to continue with the shops after Shirley left, but in the meantime we started to look around for a small cottage in which to retire.

RETIREMENT AT LAST

It was early 1980 and we were still looking for the right cottage in which to retire. We wanted a small home that was easy to follow as we both wished to travel.

Jean being very keen to do so, as she had joined WAAF in the war with the idea of being able to travel. This she never did, spending all of the five war years in England. I can tell you why she never got abroad, she worked as a telephone operator under flying control on all the major airports from Carlisle to Duxford, and she knew all the fighter pilots by name that you still read about in war books of that period. I know she would have been such a good member of staff, and so very conscientious, that they would never let her go abroad.

We heard about our present home through Shirley, and moved in on February 11th 1980. We continued to run the shop for a further year, commuting daily from Glusburn.

We then sold the shop to our nephew and his wife, going back daily to help them for a further year to let them get the feel of the business. We finally retired at the end of 1982. That means I started work at the age of 24 and finished at the age of 57.

My accountant told me to sign on unemployment until I was 60 to get my stamps credited for my future pension. I went to Keighley to the labour office, entered the building to find I was the only white person in the building. While waiting in the queue to sign on, I noticed everyone in front of me was then going to a second window. After getting a piece of paper at the first window, they all collected various amounts of money.

When it came to my turn, I signed a form but the lady gave me no other form. I said, 'Do I not get any money?' The lady said, 'You are not entitled to any.' I replied, 'I have more stamps on my card than all the 18 people in the queue put together.' She said, 'I'm sorry, I do not make the rules.' I replied, 'Alright, don't bother I will go back to my old trade.' With this remark, she sat up and started to take notice, saying, 'Oh Mr Holmes I did not know you had a trade, I will see what I can do for you, what is your trade?' I took a deep breath and said 'POACHER.'

Author on holiday in Malta for celebration of the island's fiftieth anniversary of being awarded the George Cross.

A short while later, I received a letter saying that my stamps would be credited and not to go again. I often wonder if she is still looking for a poacher's vacancy in Keighley.

I was pleased when I was allowed to keep a few pigeons and then some poultry in the field at the back of Town End Farm, this gave me something to do in my spare time, and I flew a dozen or so pigeons in Silsden and District Flying Club and Cowling Homing Society for a few years.

During this time, Jean and I were going on holidays to Scotland, Holland and Belgium, and were enjoying every minute of our retirement.

Later, I moved the few pigeons I had to the garden behind our cottage. I started to show them again for the next few years. I did well at showing, winning the show trophy five years out of seven at Cowling. I won the show trophy at Cowling, Skipton and Silsden all in the same year, something I think no other fancier has achieved.

Ernest Petty, Jean's brother and my best man, and his wife Dorothy, Jean's bridesmaid, came to live in the cottage next door to us in May 1988. We were so glad to have them near to us after all these years apart, with them living in Buckinghamshire.

Jean and I continue to have days out in the Dales and also started to visit the island of Malta. The first time I saw this island was 50 years earlier, when we sailed into harbour for safety before continuing our journey to Sicily during the war. We have since been many times and are getting as well known there as some of the residents.

Over the years we have tried to take part in many events going on around us. This has helped us in some way to have a younger and modern outlook for our age. We have served on all sorts of committees together, and between us taken up many officer positions of president, secretary, treasurer and delegates to some of the organisations I can remember. To name but a few: St Peter's Church, Addingham; The Memorial Hall; British Legion; Bolton Abbey Cricket Club; Women's Institute; OAP organisations; and of course the pigeon clubs where we both held positions up to federation and combines level, Jean being one of the few women to do so in those early years.

My last few words must be about Edward and Robert, our grandchildren. When they were born, we wondered if we would live to see them go to school. Yet in a few months' time we will see them both become teenagers. They will then soon be young men in their own right.

Jean and I are now looking forward to reaching our golden wedding on August 9th 1999.

So to sum up, my life would be:

I HAVE WORKED A BIT
I HAVE TRAVELLED A LOT
I HAVE CRIED A BIT

I HAVE LAUGHED A LOT
I HAVE EARNED A BIT
I HAVE SPENT A LOT.

SO WHEN I SPEND UP
I STARTED WITH 'NOWT'
I SHALL FINISH WITH 'NOWT'.

ADDINGHAM AS IT USED TO BE

The period about 1930 to 1940 I liked best of all, as Addingham was just one big, happy family. You will see overleaf the names of these families that I can remember. If I have left anyone out I am sorry.

Some names, like my own, Holmes, had about ten families living in the village. When you started to check, you were related to over half the village. This was wonderful until you did something wrong, then your father had found out before you got home, worse luck.

No new housing had taken place at this time but we had many more houses in the old part of the village than there are now. Houses that have been pulled down since then are:

> North Street, both sides
> Burnside Cottages
> Main Street, above Bolton and Emmotts Mill
> Brumfit Hill
> Main Street, above the Sailor Hotel
> Main Street, opposite Independent Row
> Houses behind Townhead Mill
> School Lane, houses on left
> Bolton Road, Nos. 1 to 17
> Malt Kiln Yard
> Plum Tree Hill

It was a busy village in those days, with well over twenty shops in the Main Street, all making a living, some remaining in the same family for generations.

Hundreds of extra people were transported in by bus from Yeadon, Guiseley and Silsden districts to work in the mills. At lunchtime, between

12.00 and 1.00pm, the Main Street was heaving with people from the mill and there were long queues at all the fish shops, baker's or butcher's and others selling food.

Transport in the village was a mixture of everything, horse and float for milk deliveries, parcels came to the railway station and were distributed on the horse and cart owned by the railway, stabled at the Crown. Wood, if required, came by Brear's donkey and cart. Buses were operated by the West Yorkshire Road Car Company. You could travel from Addingham by rail, steam of course, so we had in the village a good service for everyone.

The finest sight to me was that of two large railway engines, coupled together, standing on the bridge over Main Street waiting for passengers getting on a trip train of about ten coaches going to Morecambe. When the signal was given for it to depart, the steam, smoke and sparks from the two engines flying around trying to pull away up the hill towards Bolton Abbey, then the roar like thunder when the drivers opened up the regulators fully, was the greatest sight to see. One I will never forget but, alas, is never to be seen again.

The bypass was talked about at this time and all sorts of plans had been produced to take it from Corner Stones to Heathness, round the north of the village. Though at this time I do not think anyone really wanted it; not the traders, farmers or land and property owners.

Now it has been built, after many very differing routes had been put forward over the years. Has it really done anything positive for the village? This is my opinion, and many of the old villagers will say certainly not. It is very doubtful from the traders' point of view, with only a few of the shops still surviving today.

It appears to have caused more problems than it has solved.

ADDINGHAM FAMILIES

Adams	Dodd	Horsman	Smith
Appleyard	Douglas	Hudson	Snowdon
Ashton	Dove	Hustwick	Spencer
Attack	Ellis	Johnson	Stapleton
Barrett	Emmott	Kettlewell	Steels
Benson	England	Lancaster	Storey
Berry	Ettenfield	Lawrence	Sutcliffe
Blackburn	Fletcher	Lemon	Tearne
Blagborough	Flint	Lister	Thackray
Blaythorne	Foster	Lodge	Thompson
Bolton	Gill	Lowcock	Tomlin
Bradley	Golding	Mason	Townson
Brear	Green	Milburn	Walker
Buckle	Hadley	Mills	Wadeson
Burdock	Hall	Milner	Wall
Bye	Hargrave	Morris	Wallbank
Clayton	Hargreaves	Oddy	Watts
Cockcroft	Harrison	Partner	Watson
Cockshott	Hatton	Petty	Whitaker
Cook	Henderson	Readshaw	Whitehead
Crabtree	Hewerdine	Ridley	Whiteoak
Davies	Hillbeck	Rishworth	Whitham
Dean	Hodgson	Robinson	Wilkinson
Dickinson	Holmes	Roe	Woodhouse
Dinsdale	Hollingdrake	Shackleton	Wroe
Dixon	Holloway	Simpson	Wynn

TRIBUTES

I would like to write a short tribute to a few people whose company I have had the pleasure and enjoyment of for hundreds of happy hours over the years.

Aunt Eva

Even though she was my godmother and my second mother, we had some great times together. Even allowing for her poor health, she had a funny side to her that many people did not see or appreciate. When you found that side of her she was at her very best.

Uncle Fred

He was the finest self-made man I have known. He only went to school, the old school above the library in Addingham, from the age of six and left at the age of 11. Yet he taught himself to play the piano; to drive a coach and horses; drive a car, the third in Addingham; was a professional sprinter and a self-taught businessman, and during all this time he was subsidising his living as a poacher. He knew every bird or animal he saw in the countryside and could catch most of them with a self-made trap or snare.

In later years, when I knew him, he was a great entertainer and the finest raconteur I have ever known. He was 43 years my senior; what I would have given to have been born in his generation.

Eddie Hudson

Eddie was one of the kindest men I have had the pleasure of knowing. He was only married for a few weeks, then this broke up when he went to Burma in the war for five years. Yet he had no bitterness in him and got on building a new life.

I had the pleasure of working with him for over 18 years, both full and part time, and not a wrong word between us. He remained on his own for the rest of his life, but this did not stop him doing jobs and good turns for anyone.

Eddie never seemed to get the luck he so deserved; he died only two years after retiring.

Tommy Crabtree

Tommy and myself represented pigeon clubs as delegates for more years than I care to remember. We were on every committee going, from club to race committee, to show committee, delegates to federation and combines, the length and breadth of northwest Yorkshire.

Tommy was only a working chap, but his knowledge and flair for pigeon administration was outstanding. He always voted for the benefit of the sport and not the individual. If more people had taken Tommy's way, pigeon racing would be in a better shape than it is today.

We travelled home together from meetings at all hours of the day and night, he always had a tale to tell and was very,v ery good company. I enjoyed every minute with him.

He was a good few years older than me, yet died only about two years ago.

Joe Hargrave

I knew Joe all his life, being a bit older than him. It was not until we were both married and had families that we became lifelong friends. By then Joe had his own business, and I would help him from time to time with the painting of houses if he got a large contract to paint a row of new houses, which he did fairly often.

He taught me all I know about painting and I still consider myself well above the usual DIY standard, thanks to him.

Though it was at showing pigeons and then rabbits that he was in a class of his own. When we were showing pigeons together, his lofts were painted inside with white gloss paint that could be cleaned down daily and not a speck of dirt could be found anywhere.

You, or even someone who did not understand pigeons, could pick his birds out anytime in the show pen, they had not a speck of dirt or a feather out of place, from the beak of the bird to its toenails.

Of all the many pigeon showmen I have known, he was miles better than them all, only one word would describe him: 'Perfectionist'.

Though as I have noticed often, all the great men seem to die so young, as did Joe, at the very early age of 61.

Jean Holmes

My wife, lifetime partner and best friend. The last words must be about Jean, but what do you say that has not already been said many times in 50 years of marriage?

Other than if we could start all over again, I would do nothing different but share my life with you.

On August 9th 2009 Mum and Dad
celebrated 60 years together,
their diamond wedding anniversary,
quietly with their family at home.

THE STORY CONTINUES...

Shirley divorced in 1998, this brought its own problems for Robert and Jean continued to see their grandchildren Edward and Robert but due to circumstances beyond Shirley's control she did not see them for quite a number of years.

Robert and Jean gave her updates but these did not in any way make up for not seeing her boys. She knew they were alright as her parents saw to that, having them come for visits and tea.

Shirley remarried and had a daughter, Alice Clara, who looks just like her Mum, with long blond hair, and Robert often confused the two as the years went on.

In May 2001, Shirley and her husband John moved to a bungalow in Silsden, with room for her parents to move into should they have wanted. Robert said it was the only thing that Jean and Robert fell out about, he wanted to stay in the cottage in Glusburn while Jean wanted to move nearer to Shirley.

Jean won, just one of the times when she put her foot down, Jean didn't often do this but when she did, Robert took notice.

In 2004, Jean and Robert moved into the Grannie wing. Once they had moved in even Robert had to agree it was the right thing to have done as they were close to Shirley and of course could see Alice who they both adored as she was so much like their daughter. They could spend time in the garden and even decided to have Shirleys cat Felix live with them, this was unbelievable as Robert had not liked cats, always preferring dogs.

In 2008 they moved for six months to a cottage near Hawes, on a friends farm while Shirley and John had major renovations done to convert the bungalow into a house. Robert and Jean loved

Hawes and went most weeks during their retirement and as long as he could drive, staying there was like a second home. They loved to go to the café for lunch and get shopping from the stalls in the market hall; with going regularly the locals became like their extended family as everyone knew them.

Retirement was good and life could be taken at a gentler pace.

Robert and Jean made a prediction when Edward was born about not seeing him finish education, well not only did they see him finish school but they saw him move in with his future wife and daughter Milly Rose, they became great grandparents in 2010 when Charlie Thomas was born on 29th December.

In February 2010 Jean became poorly and was diagnosed to be suffering from Dementia. Her health quickly deteriorated and she moved into the Nursing Home at the top of the road, Robert visited her daily until she passed away in October of that year.

Robert was never the same, life went on but without Jean he had lost his focus, he was not one for family gatherings and parties, that was Jeans scene not his. Robert did not go to Edward and Sues Wedding but stayed safe at home. Robert always preferred a quiet life.

In November 2012 Edward had another son, Freddie James.

Roberts grandson Robert in the meantime had met his future wife Liz and they married in May 2013. Robert was invited but again he declined preferring just to stay safe at home.

Robert continued to live with Shirley until his health started to fail and he needed 24 hour care, finally moving into the Nursing where his beloved Jean had lived, he too suffered from a form of dementia and simply, in his own way, drifted from this world quietly and peacefully with Shirley at his side in the early hours of Thursday 7th August 2014.

Robert, in his fashion, had been successful in many ways, he survived through hard times, through war and yes through the good times of life lived to the full, but in one sense he achieved something to which most of us can only ever aspire to dream... he had worked for less years than he had been retired.

www.ingramcontent.com/pod-product-compliance
Lightning Source LLC
Chambersburg PA
CBHW041718090426
42739CB00018B/3469